JOHN WITTICH

D0645904

Discovering London Street Names

SHIRE PUBLICATIONS LTD

Contents

The cover illustration is 'Pillory, Charing Cross' by Thomas Rowlandson (1809).

All photographs are by Cadbury Lamb, except that on page 4, which is the copyright of John and Andrew Wittich.

British Library Cataloguing in Publication Data. Wittich, John. Discovering London Street Names. – 3rd ed. 1. Street names – England – London. I. Title. 914.2'1'0014. ISBN 0-7478-0309-9.

Published in 2003 by Shire Publications Ltd, Cromwell House, Church Street, Princes Risborough, Buckinghamshire HP27 9AA, UK. Website: www.shirebooks.co.uk
Copyright © 1977 and 1996 by John Wittich. First published 1977, reprinted 1983; second edition 1990; third expanded edition 1996; reprinted 2003. Number 225 in the Discovering series. ISBN 0 7478 0309 9.

Printed in Great Britain by CIT Printing Services Ltd, Press Buildings, Merlins Bridge, Haverfordwest, Pembrokeshire SA61 1XF.

Introduction

It is a strange fact that there are no roads under the control of the City of London, although there are many streets, lanes, alleys and places which bear just a single name, like Cheapside. The explanation for this is that all Roman roads were tree-lined whereas the streets were not; London's street plan is of Roman origin, but the fine roadways disappeared in the later congestion. Medieval London became a veritable maze of small alleys and lanes busy with people and traffic.

The medieval streets and lanes were often full of garbage, and there was little or no chance of its being cleared away. It is said that some of the narrowest byways were so littered that it was impossible even to ride a horse along them. Houses were built with upper storeys projecting to such an extent that they appeared to meet at roof level when viewed from the street. Housemaids cleaning the upper rooms and making the beds would throw the night slops out of the windows down into the street. This habit has always been given as the reason why a gentleman will walk on the outside edge of the pavement when accompanying or passing a lady.

The medieval street scene was a constantly changing and colourful one, with pilgrims rubbing shoulders with citizens, citizens stopping and staring perhaps at a procession on its way to some city function, knights on their way to the king at the Tower of London, bishops, priests, monks, nuns and lay people all going about their everyday business amongst the hustle and bustle of a wealthy, commercially oriented city.

All this was swept away in 1666 by the Great Fire of London, and although there were schemes for a planned rebuilding of the City of London after the catastrophe none made any progress. Indeed, until the aftermath of the Second World War (1939-45), which devastated parts of the City and elsewhere, the only town-planner to make any impression on the spreading metropolis was John Nash (1752-1835), royal architect of George IV, in the late eighteenth and early nineteenth centuries.

The late twentieth century brought its changes, opening out new vistas to reveal the old amongst the modern. Buildings of unprecedented height stretch upwards and whole streets have disappeared as plans proliferate for the development of each and every site.

Many London street names are reminders of taverns and inns which stood there in the past. Innumerable Swans, Bulls, Bells and other such names recall previous occupants of the site. Fitzstephen, a twelfth-century writer, said that the two greatest perils of London were fires and excessive drinking.

The duplication of street names such as High Street can be simplified by prefixing the name of the locality, for example, Clapham High Street. But such popular names as King, of which there are over forty, and Clarence, with some thirty in all, can be confusing. Kings and queens have left their mark, and men of literature have made a substantial contribution to the street map, which includes twenty-four Miltons, eleven Tennysons, twelve Shakespeares, five Brownings and four Dickenses. Strange names can still be found and some, like XX Place in East London, defy explanation; but other charming names, like Of Alley, have succumbed and been changed.

The erection of stone tablets showing the name at the end of a street began in the seventeenth century. One of the earliest still *in situ* is at Devereux Court and dates from 1676.

Dozens of former villages have become absorbed into present-day London, and each has many streets that recall the history of the area. This book includes a selection of street names from the lost villages of London, as well as many from the City, from the West End and from the surrounding neighbourhoods. The names of the villages themselves are interesting and some of these, too, have been included.

One of London's oldest street-name signs can be seen at
Marsham Street, SW1

London street names

Abbey Orchard Street, SW1
All monasteries had to be self-sufficient in providing for themselves and their guests. Fresh fruit from the abbey's orchard was a
most important part of their diet. The area was built up in the
second half of the seventeenth century.

Abbotsbury Road, W14
This is a reminder of the area's previous connection with Abingdon
Abbey in Oxfordshire. See under Abingdon Road.

Abchurch Lane, Abchurch Yard, EC4
Wren's church of St Mary Abchurch was once known as Upchurch
from its position on the rising ground.

Abingdon Road, Abingdon Villas, W8
Geoffrey de Vere gave land here to the Abbey of Abingdon on his
death in 1109. Because of his bequest this part of Kensington
became known as Abbot's Kensington and the parish church as St
Mary Abbots.

Abingdon Street, SW1
Here lived Lord Mounteagle's sister, Mary Abingdon, the lady
who wrote the fatal letter that led to the uncovering of the plot to
blow up Parliament in 1605. Its earlier name is recorded as Dirty
Lane, and it was formerly the site of the town house of the Earl of
Abingdon.

Adam Street, WC2
One of the streets in the Adelphi, which was built by the Adam
brothers beside the river in the eighteenth century. Born in Edinburgh, they brought their style of architecture and interior decora-
tion to London, where their work is still much admired today.

Addle Hill, off Carter Lane, EC4
Here stood the royal palace of King Athelstan (Adelstan) in Saxon
times.

Adelaide Street, WC2
Named after Queen Adelaide (1792-1849), who was born Princess
Adelaide of Saxe-Coburg and Meiningen and in 1818 married the
Duke of Clarence. He succeeded to the throne as William IV in
1830 and died in 1837.

Adelphi, WC2

The Greek word *adelphi* means 'brothers' and it was the Adam brothers who created what was one of the most fashionable places to live in eighteenth-century London. Built on the banks of the river, the cellars, or the 'Arches' as they were popularly known, carried the weight of the houses above. Most of the houses have long since been pulled down and other buildings have replaced them, but follow Lower John Street and you will find yourself on a public roadway, 'underneath the Arches', leading out on to a modern embankment.

Agar Street, WC2

During the rebuilding of the Strand in the nineteenth century the First Commissioner of Woods and Forests was a certain Agar-Ellis, who is commemorated here.

Akenside Road, NW3

Mark Akenside, the eighteenth-century poet, lived in Hampstead. This is the only street named after him in London.

The Albany, W1

A curious survival from the eighteenth century, the nucleus of these buildings consisted of three residences, occupied in part by the third Earl of Sutherland, who converted them into one house. In 1770 the first Lord Melbourne bought the present house but later exchanged it with the Duke of York and Albany, son of George III and the 'Grand Old Duke of York' of the nursery rhyme, for Dover House in Whitehall. In 1803 it was first let out as chambers, and it has become a private and very select residence. It should be noted that admission is only granted to the residents and their guests – it is not a public thoroughfare.

Albemarle Street, W1

Following the restoration of the monarchy in 1660, the popular General Monk was rewarded with land here by the grateful king, Charles II. The general's second son, who succeeded to his father's title of Duke of Albemarle in the late seventeenth century, had a magnificent house here, but, like the surrounding streets, Albemarle Street was developed by Sir Thomas Bond.

Albert Embankment, SE1

Part of the protective wall erected along the riverbank to the designs of Sir Joseph Bazalgette in the 1870s, it commemorates Queen Victoria's husband Prince Albert of Saxe-Coburg-Gotha (1819-61).

Aldermanbury, EC2

Here, at the centre of Saxon London, the aldermen (elder statesmen of the wards) met in their 'bury' (house), before the building of the first guildhall.

Aldersgate Street, EC1
Leading from one of the oldest gates in the city wall – hence *alder* (older) gate – the roadway once led to the north of England and Scotland. It was through this gateway that James I of England (James VI of Scotland) entered to claim the English throne after the death of Elizabeth I in 1603. John Milton came to live here after his marriage to Mary Powell 'because there were few streets in London more free from noise than Aldersgate'.

Aldgate High Street, EC3
The old, eastern gate of the City of London was first built in Roman times and led to the east coast, Essex and Suffolk. The High Street was the main thoroughfare for the local community.

Aldwych, WC2
The name may be formed from the Anglo-Saxon words *wic* (a village or town) and *ald* (old), thus meaning 'old town', but there is a possible alternative derivation from the Norse *vic* (a creek or harbour). The church of St Clement Danes nearby reminds us of the small colony of Danes who settled here in the ninth and tenth centuries. The houses and alleyways of Aldwych were demolished early in the twentieth century to make way for a main road.

Alexander Square

Alexander Square, SW3
This well-preserved Victorian square is named after the family of W. H.

Alexander, whose gift to London in 1896, the National Portrait Gallery, houses portraits of men and women who have influenced British history.

Alleyn Road, SE21
Edward Alleyn, actor and local benefactor, was born in 1566, in the parish of St Botolph's Bishopsgate in the City of London, and died in 1626. His body lies in the chapel of Dulwich College, his 'College of God's Gift'.

Alwyne Square, N1
The Marquess of Northampton's family have long and distinguished associations with the borough of Islington, and their surname is recorded here.

Amen Court, EC4
Under the shadow of St Paul's, the cathedral's canons and prebendaries live in these houses, which date, in part, from the late seventeenth century. Here in medieval processions, reciting their rosaries around the cathedral precincts they would, by tradition, say 'Amen'.

America Square, EC3
Built between 1761 and 1774, just before the signing of the treaty that gave the United States of America its independence, the houses were occupied by North American merchants. Baron de Rothschild lived at number 14 during the nineteenth century but the house was destroyed by bombs during the Second World War.

Andre Street, E8
Major John Andre was unjustly hanged as a spy in 1780 when he was captured while on a secret mission for Benedict Arnold in the American War of Independence. He was born at Pond House, Clapton.

Angel Mews, N1
This cul-de-sac mews is behind the former site of the Angel Inn.

Apothecary Street, EC4
Halls of the worshipful companies of the City have dwindled in number over the years and only a few dozen remain. That of the Society of Apothecaries, dating from 1670 and 1786, has a very beautiful main hall panelled in black oak and stands at the end of this street in Blackfriars Lane.

Argyll Place, Argyll Street, W1

The mansion of the Duke of Argyll formerly stood here on the east side of the street.

Arlington Street, SW1

First built in 1689 on ground belonging to the Earl of Arlington, a member of Charles II's Cabal ministry, the street was for a short time the home of Lord and Lady Nelson. The final quarrel between them, after which Lady Nelson left never to return, took place here. Sir Robert Walpole and his son Horace both lived at number 5 during the eighteenth century.

Arnos Grove, N14; Arnos Road, N11

These roads were built on land owned by the Arnold family.

Artillery Lane, E1

Here was the practising ground for the City Trained Bands, founded in the year of the Great Armada, 1588. Cannons were placed at the end to prevent wheeled traffic from entering the lane. It is said that they once formed part of the armament of the volunteers. Stow records that there was a large close here, where crossbow makers used to play shooting games. Pepys, in his diary, writes of the 'old artillery ground' near Spitalfields.

Artillery Row, SW1

This was outside the old city of Westminster where the artillery gunners practised.

Ashmole Street, SW8

The founder of the Ashmolean Museum in Oxford, Elias Ashmole (1617-92), lived in Lambeth and lies buried in St Mary's churchyard 'hard by the palace'.

Aubert Park, Aubert Road, N5

Lieutenant-Colonel Alexander Aubert (1730-1804), a notable soldier and astronomer, lived in Highbury Manor House.

Audley Street, North and South, W1

Stretching from Oxford Street in the north to Curzon Street in the south, and passing through Grosvenor Square, these streets take their names from Hugh Audley, a seventeenth-century moneylender and local landowner.

Austin Friars, EC2

One of the many monastic orders in the City during the middle ages, the Augustinian Friars were established here in 1253 by Humphrey de Bohun, Earl of Hereford and Essex. At the dissolution of the monasteries in the sixteenth century the nave of the church was set aside for the use of Dutch refugees. Today the Dutch community still worships at the church, rebuilt after bombing in the Second World War.

Ave Maria Lane, EC4

This is part of the pre-Reformation processional route followed on such feast days as Corpus Christi, when the rosary was recited round the precincts of St Paul's. *Ave Maria* is translated as 'Hail Mary'.

Avondale Park, W11

The park was formed in 1892, the year that the future Edward VII's elder son, the Duke of Clarence and Avondale, died of influenza. It has been suggested that the Duke was the notorious Jack the Ripper, although substantial evidence has never been established.

Baker Street, NW1 and W1

Speculative builders in the seventeenth and eighteenth centuries produced a number of streets and squares around London. One such was Sir Edward Baker, of Runston in Dorset.

Ball Court, off Cornhill by number 38, EC3

First mentioned in 1799, the court's most famous premises is Simpson's Chop House, established in 1757. Of the origin of the name nothing is known for certain; perhaps it was merely the landowner's own name.

Balls Pond Road, N1

In the late seventeenth century the pond on John Ball's land was well stocked with fowl provided for the gentlemen visiting his tavern to shoot.

Balmes Road, N1

Two brothers, Spanish merchants, built their house here, calling it Balmes House. It later became a private asylum and one patient in the eighteenth century, was Mary Lamb. Her brother, Charles Lamb, author and essayist, was a constant visitor here during her stay.

Bankside, Southwark, SE1

On the bank of the river Thames in the liberty of the Clink, Southwark, this area was notorious in the seventeenth and eighteenth centuries.

Barbauld Road, N16
A great beauty when she was young, Anna Letitia Barbauld (1743-1825), daughter of John Aikin, retained her charms to her last days. But she is remembered today for her literary work of poems and prose including *Early Lessons* and *Hymns in Prose for Children*. She was buried in Stoke Newington churchyard, and a memorial to her was erected on the walls of Newington Green Chapel.

Barbican, EC1
A barbican was a high tower built on a mound, from where a guard could keep watch over the city and the surrounding countryside. Dryden wrote:
'A watch-tower once, but now, so fate ordains,
Of all the pile an empty name remains.'
So by the seventeenth century it was disused and in ruins.

Barnard Inn, EC1
One of the numerous inns of court which have ceased to function but which retain the name of a former owner. The inn was originally founded by Dr John Mackworth, Dean of Lincoln, but was later bought by Barnard, whose name it still bears.

Bartholomew Close, EC1
In 1123 Rahere, a prebendary of St Paul's, returned from Rome, where he had been on a pilgrimage to St Peter's shrine, and began to build St Bartholomew's Hospital. On the south side of the church were the cloisters and domestic quarters of the monks.

Bartholomew Lane, EC2
At one corner of the lane stood the church of St Bartholomew Exchange, taking its suffix from its proximity to the Royal Exchange. Miles Coverdale, translator of the first complete English Bible, was rector here and when the church was demolished in 1849 his remains were transferred to the church of St Magnus the Martyr, by London Bridge.

Barton Street, SW1
A former pupil of Westminster School, Barton Booth became a famous actor in the seventeenth and eighteenth centuries. His family owned land in the City of Westminster.

Basinghall Street, EC2
The Basings were a family of some importance who had their hall

11

(house) here in the middle ages. They are also remembered in the name of a ward of the City. One of the family, Solomon Basing, was Mayor of London in 1216.

Battersea
The name is derived from Patricsey Island, meaning 'Peter's island', for it was owned by the abbey of St Peter at Westminster, whose monks used the place as a convalescent home.

Battle Bridge Road, NW1
Although historians cannot agree as to the exact site of the battle in AD 61 in which Boadicea, queen of the Iceni tribe, defeated the Romans, evidence which points to this area has been found during excavations.

Baylis Road, SE1
Lilian Baylis (1874-1937), niece of the famous theatrical figure Emma Cons, was her partner in the venture which led to the establishment of the Old Vic theatre and went on to make it 'the home of Shakespeare'.

Bayswater Road, W2
Baynardus or Bainiardus, an associate of William the Conqueror (1027-87), is mentioned in documents dated 1653 which show a common field of Paddington as being near 'Baynards Watering'. George Francis Train, an American, ran the world's first tramway along the road from Lancaster Gate to the Marble Arch in 1860. The line was launched with a banquet in St James's church hall, but the tramlines gave rise to so much complaint that they were soon removed. Train returned to America, where he died after trying to live on a diet of peanuts.

Bear Gardens, SE1
Bear-baiting in these gardens continued long after the nearby theatres had been destroyed by the Puritans. The animals were starved for several days before being tied to a post in the centre of the arena. Dogs were then set on them while the spectators gambled on the outcome.

Bear Street, WC2
The Neville family were local landowners. Their heraldic badge was a bear and ragged staff.

Beaufort Street, SW3
The street follows the course of the avenue that led from the riverside to the first Duke of Beaufort's seventeenth-century house, which was built on the site of Sir Thomas More's home.

Bedfordbury, WC2
A 'bury' was a large house, and the Dukes of Bedford had such a mansion here.

Bedford Park, W4
An estate was built here on land that had been owned by one Tubbs Bedford in the late seventeenth century.

Bedford Square, WC1
Estates developed by the landed gentry in the eighteenth century invariably recorded their names and titles and the Bedford estate is no exception. Laid out to the design of Thomas Leverton between 1775 and 1780, this is one of London's unspoilt squares.

Bedford Street, WC2
John Russell, first Earl of Bedford, was given land in the area of Covent Garden by Charles II (1630-85) and engaged Inigo Jones, the noted architect, to design the streets and houses here.

Belgrave Square, SW1
The square, laid out by Thomas Cubitt between 1825 and 1828, covers some ten acres and is named after the village in Cheshire

Belgrave Square

that forms one of the secondary titles of the landowner, the Duke of Westminster.

Bell Yard, Carter Lane, EC4
While staying at the Bell, Richard Quiney wrote the only letter to William Shakespeare to survive. It is preserved at Shakespeare's birthplace at Stratford-upon-Avon, Warwickshire.

Bell Yard, off Strand, WC2
Here stood the Bell hostel, owned by the Knights Templar. They used land nearby to train soldiers for the defence of the holy places of Palestine.

Belsize Park, Belsize Lane, NW3
A popular tea place was founded in the grounds of Belsize House and was a fashionable resort in the eighteenth century.

Benets Hill, EC4
First mentioned in the early twelfth century, St Benet's (Benedict's) church was rebuilt by Sir Christopher Wren after the Great Fire. The hill winds round the church, leading to Queen Victoria Street.

Berkeley Square, W1
The square was planned in 1698 on the site of the gardens of Berkeley House, which had been the home of Lord Berkeley of Stratton.

Berkeley Street, W1
John Evelyn records in his diary on 12th June 1684 that he went to Berkeley Gardens to advise on the laying out of the two streets there. The work was being carried out in the grounds of the house of John Berkeley, the youngest son of Sir Maurice Berkeley.

Bevis Marks, EC2
A corruption of 'Buries Marks', meaning Bury's Limits. It marks the limits of the mansion and grounds of the London home of the Abbot of Bury St Edmunds in Suffolk.

Billingsgate, EC3
One of the oldest fish markets in Europe, Billingsgate was founded in 1699. Its name is said to have come from an ancient king of the Britons, Beling or Biling. Biling's gate was the entrance to a hithe or dock, and on his death his ashes were placed in an urn on the gate.

Billiter Street, Billiter Square, EC3

At the end of the middle ages there were over 120 churches in London and in consequence the bellfounders' guild was a prosperous one. Its members were called *belzeters*, from which term 'billiter' is derived. It was here that they made their bells and tuned them.

Birchin Lane, EC3

The first builder and owner of houses in this lane was Birchervere, who gave his name to it. However, Ekwall, in his book on the derivation of the street names of the City, based on the streets at the time of John Stow (1525-1605), says that the word comes from the fact that the barbers made their home here and is, therefore, a derivation of the word 'barber'. Birchin Lane was once subject to the Metropolitan Streets Act of 1867, whereby it was forbidden to carry any object more than thirty-six feet long or eight feet six inches wide along it. Neither might you unload coal on the footway or drive a vehicle drawn by more than four horses on the roadway.

Birdcage Walk, SW1

The walk which runs alongside St James's Park owes its name to the aviary owned by Charles II, which is said to have contained many exotic birds, including a crane with a wooden leg and another bird that would eat hot coals.

Bishopsgate, EC2

Erkenwald, Bishop of London from 675 to 693, built a gate in the north-east sector of the city wall, and it became known as Bishopsgate. A mitre, the distinctive head-dress of a bishop, is still prominently displayed on the buildings on the site of the original gate. A toll of one stick was exacted on the bishop's behalf from all carts bringing wood into the city.

Blackfriars Lane, EC4

Originally established in about 1221 near Lincoln's Inn, the Dominicans, or Black Friars, moved here some fifty years later.

Black Prince Road, SE1

Edward III gave his son Edward, the Black Prince (1330-76), the manor of Vauxhall and Kennington.

Blomfield Road, W9

This was named after a nineteenth-century Bishop of London,

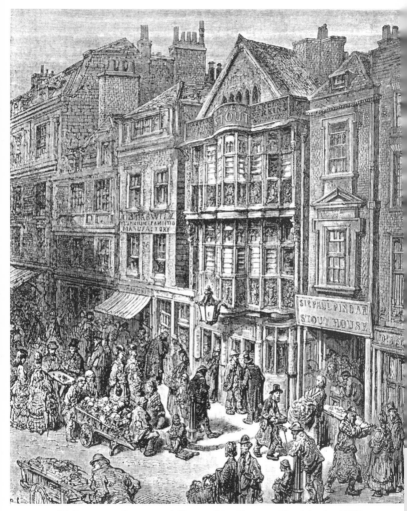

Bishopsgate Street as delineated by Gustave Doré in the 1870s

Charles James Blomfield (1786-1857), who is also remembered for his classical studies and for the two hundred new churches consecrated in London during the twenty-eight years he was bishop.

16

Bloomsbury Square, Bloomsbury Place, Bloomsbury Way, WC1
The ownership of manors and estates often changes and a thirteenth-century example was the Berwick of Tottenhale, which was sold to William Blemund. The name of his manor, or bury, has come down to the present as Bloomsbury.

Blue Boar Yard, off St James's Street, SW1
All that remains of the eighteenth-century Blue Boar inn is the stables behind.

Boadicea Street, N1
Boadicea, queen of the Iceni, made her mark on British history, particularly with the razing of the city of London in AD 61. Here is the site of one of the skirmishes.

Bolt Court, Fleet Street, EC4
Dr Johnson lived, until he died in 1784, in this court, which takes its name from a former owner of the site. The family rebus, a representation of a name in pictures, was a bolt in a tun, that is a bolt, shot from a crossbow, piercing a barrel – a tun. Another rebus of the family can be seen at the church of St Bartholomew the Great, Smithfield, in Prior Bolton's window.

Bolton Street, W1
Described by Hatton in the early eighteenth century as being the 'most westerly street in London between the road to Knightsbridge, south, and the Fields, north', the street was formed in 1699 and takes its name from its previous owner's family.

Bond Street, New and Old, W1
As London grew in the seventeenth century, speculative builders bought up land on the outskirts, demolished the large houses which stood there and developed the areas into well laid-out streets. Between 1686 and 1716 Sir Thomas Bond of Peckham, a former Comptroller to the Royal Household, built streets on land where Clarendon House in Piccadilly once stood.

Borough High Street, SE1
From Roman times until the sixteenth century Southwark was a separate entity from the city of London and is recorded as a 'burgh' or 'borough' at the end of the ninth century. The main roads from the south-east joined to form its High Street, which led to London Bridge at its northern extremity.

Boswell Court, Boswell Street, WC1
James Boswell (1740-95), the diarist, friend and biographer of Dr
Samuel Johnson, lived in Holborn for two years.

Botolph Lane, Botolph Alley, EC3
At the end of the lane, on the riverbank, St Botolph's church was
destroyed by the Great Fire of London in 1666. It was not rebuilt.
In the lane also stood the only City church dedicated to England's
patron saint, St George, but it too has long since vanished.

Bourne Street, SW1
Formerly called Westbourne Street, from the nearby river, the name was
changed to avoid confusion with other streets using the river's name.

Bouverie Street, EC4
Much land in the City became available after the dissolution of
monastic establishments in the sixteenth century. The land of the
White Friars was acquired by the Bouverie family.

Bow Lane, EC4
Shoemakers' shops were once found in this lane and in Cordwainer
Street, but later they moved away and the street became Bow Lane
after the church of St Mary-le-Bow which stands at its head. The
'bows' are the arches upon which the church is built.

Bowling Green Lane, EC1
At one time it was known as Featherbed Lane; it takes its present
name from the number of bowling greens here in the sixteenth
century, as recorded by John Stow in his *Survay of the Cities of
London and Westminster*, first published in 1598.

Bowman's Mews, Bowman's Place, N7
Archery was a popular pastime in Elizabethan days and facilities
were often set up in the outlying villages.

Bow Street, WC2
Shaped like a longbow, the street was laid out in the fourth decade
of the seventeenth century. Queen Victoria ordered that the lights
outside the famous police station in this street be changed from
blue to white — the only ones in London. William Wycherley, the
dramatist, lived and died (in 1716) in a house on the site of the
present Royal Opera House, and he was visited here by Charles II.

Bread Street, EC4
John Milton was born in 1608 in this street, where bakers used to

Bow Street

gather to sell their wares. The name *Bredestrate* appears in 1180 and in the *Liber Albus*, compiled in the fifteenth century, it says that no baker shall sell his bread 'before his oven, but only in the market of the King'.

Brick Court, Temple, EC4
Within the Temple precinct, this was the first court to be built solely of brick. It dates from the seventeenth century.

Brick Street, W1
Part of this street was, until 1878, shown on maps as Engine Street, from the watermill on the banks of the river Tyburn. Other streets in the area of Mayfair were constructed of stone, but here the houses were built more cheaply of brick.

Bridewell Place, EC4
The church of St Bride (Bridget) in Fleet Street has remains of an ancient spring or well that used to attract thousands of pilgrims.

Nearby stood the Bridewell prison, given by Edward VI in the year of his death (1553) to the City Corporation as a workhouse – the earliest known – a house of correction for vagabonds and tramps.

Bridge Street, SW1
Until the eighteenth century the only bridge across the Thames in London was London Bridge. A new one was constructed here at Westminster between 1736 and 1750 at a cost of £426,650, and streets, north and south, were laid out to take the new flow of traffic.

Broad Sanctuary, SW1
In and around a medieval city could be found 'sanctuaries' – holy and protected areas. Often sited within the precincts of monastic establishments, they provided places in which thieves and vagabonds were safe from arrest, on certain conditions, usually that they confessed their crime and promised to keep the rules of the sanctuary.

Broad Street, EC2
One of the widest streets of the City in the seventeenth century, it was also a fashionable place to live at the time.

Broadway, EC4 and SW1
Both streets, one in the City and the other in Westminster, were created by the clearance of slums and alleys in the mid nineteenth century, thus forming a wide, or broad, street.

Brompton Road, SW3
Brompton denotes 'broom town', suggesting an open common where the shrub broom grew.

Brompton Road and Brompton Oratory

Brooke Road, N16

Here stood Brooke House and amongst the royal visitors here was Queen Margaret, the wife of Henry VI (1421-71). It was rebuilt in the sixteenth century by the sixth Earl of Northumberland, Henry Percy, and took its name from Fulke Greville, the first Baron Brooke (1554-1628), who lived here at the time of the reconstruction. At the end of the same century the house became a centre of intrigue for the Society of Jesus.

Brook Street, W1

One of the many streets that crosses the Tyburn brook, which runs below Mayfair near here.

Broomwood Road, West Side, Clapham Common, SW11

William Wilberforce, one of the leading figures in the movement to abolish the slave trade in the British Empire, lived in a house here called 'Broomwood'.

Brownswood Road, N16

The old manor of Brownswood covered much of the area of Hornsey and is mentioned in a survey of 1797 as Brownswood or Hornsey Wood.

Brushfield Street, E1

Thomas Brushfield, a nineteenth-century builder, gave his name to this street. He was also a distinguished member of the Metropolitan Board of Works. The Board was the predecessor of the London County Council.

Bruton Street, W1

Built about 1727, this was named after Lord Berkeley's estate in Somerset.

Buckingham Palace Road, SW1

In 1725 this was known as the coach road to Chelsea, but it later changed to its present title after the Royal Household moved into the former London residence of the Duke of Buckingham.

Buckingham Street, WC2

George Villiers, Duke of Buckingham, acquired land here in the seventeenth century and started to lay out the street plan. Other street names in the area commemorate the Duke's other personal names and titles.

The graves of Daniel Defoe and William Blake at Bunhill Fields

Bucklersbury, EC4
Here in the thirteenth and fourteenth centuries was the mansion or 'bury' of the Buckerells, a family then well-known in the City.

Bunhill Row, Bunhill Fields, EC1
Cartloads of bodies are said to have been brought here from Old St Paul's cathedral after the Great Fire, and the area became known as the Bone Hill. It later became a burial place for dissenters, and among those buried here are Mrs Samuel Wesley, mother of John and Charles Wesley, John Bunyan, William Blake and several members of the Cromwell family.

Burgon Street, EC4
Before the end of the nineteenth century this lane is shown as New Street but it was renamed Burgon Street after the Dean of Chichester, who was a frequent visitor to the City of London.

Burleigh Street, Strand, WC2
Elizabeth I's favourite statesman, William Cecil, Lord Burleigh, built a house along the Strand, which was later renamed Exeter House.

Burlington Arcade, W1
One of London's best-known and most fashionable shopping arcades, it was built, to the design of Lord George Cavendish, to prevent rubbish from being thrown over the nearby wall into the grounds of Burlington House. The total length of 585 feet contains seventy-two shops whose original rent was £18 *per annum*. Until a few years ago the arcade was patrolled by members of the 10th Hussars, whose job included keeping law and order, preventing people from carrying umbrellas through the arcade and nursemaids from pushing prams from one end to the other.

Burlington Lane, Chiswick, W4
Richard Boyle succeeded to the title of Lord Burlington at the age of ten, on the death of his father in 1704. His Temple of the Arts, built to house his collection of paintings, sculpture, books and manuscripts, and now called Chiswick House, is a superb example of English Palladian architecture.

Cadogan Pier, Cadogan Place, Cadogan Square, Cadogan Gardens, Cadogan Lane, Cadogan Street, SW1 and SW3
In the late eighteenth century the architect Henry Holland (1746-1806) leased the land from Lord Cadogan for speculative building.

Cambridge Square, W2
A local resident, the Countess of Richmond, was a generous donor to the University of Cambridge.

Camomile Street, EC3
Herbal remedies for fevers, agues and other ailments required a good supply of herbs. One of these was camomile, which grew in abundance here on the inner banks of the city wall.

Campden Hill, W8
This takes its name from Campden House, built *c*.1612 for Sir Baptist Hicks, who became the Viscount Campden of Campden in Gloucestershire.

Cannon Row, SW1
According to Stow, canons from St Stephen's Chapel of the Royal Palace of St Stephen, Westminster – commonly called the Houses of Parliament – are said to have lived here. It is also shown as Channel Row on some early maps, because the channel of the river Tyburn leads into the Thames here.

Cannon Street, EC4

Candlewick Ward of the City takes its name from the candlewrights who used to live and work there, although they were subsequently expelled and made to work in the surrounding countryside, because of constant complaints of the smell from their candle-making. The street running through the ward was renamed Cannon Street from Candlewick Street.

Capper Street, WC1

When the 'new road' (New Oxford Street, W1) was projected, among the protesters were the Capper sisters. They lived on a farm nearby and complained that the dust raised by the cattle using the road would spoil their hay. The street off Tottenham Court Road is near where their farmhouse stood.

Cardinal Cap Alley, Bankside, SE1

Leading from Bankside, the alley may take its name from the fact that Cardinal Beaufort, Bishop of Winchester from 1405 to 1447, landed here on his return from Rome after being made a cardinal by Pope Martin V. The cardinal then paraded the cap, a large broad-brimmed red hat never actually worn by the recipient, through the Precinct of the Clink then owned by the Bishops of Winchester and displayed it for all to see. Alternatively it has been suggested that the alley gets its name from the fact that the cardinal kept his own private 'tart' here, the name having been altered, over the years, from Cardinal's Tart to Cardinal's Cap. It is true that much of this area was occupied by prostitutes in the days when it was owned by the bishops.

Carey Street, WC2

Shown on maps of the late seventeenth century, when it was first developed, as leading to Carey House, the home of Sir George Carey, Carey Street was formerly the site of the bankruptcy court, hence the phrase 'going to Carey Street', referring to persons of unsound finance.

Carlisle Lane, SE1

This commemorates the former London home of the Bishops of Carlisle, used later by the Bishops of Rochester. Here Bishop St John Fisher was nearly poisoned by his cook but 'the Bishoppe eate not pottage that daie, whereby hee escaped'. Fourteen other guests were poisoned and the cook, having been convicted of the crime, was boiled to death at Smithfield.

Carlisle Street, W1

A house at one side of Soho Square was the home of the Countess of

Carlisle, whose estranged husband still maintained the family house in the square.

Carlton House Terrace, SW1
Lord Carlton owned the land here, hence the name, but it passed to his nephew Lord Burlington and was purchased from him in 1732 by Frederick, Prince of Wales. Later in the eighteenth century it passed to George IV, while he was Prince of Wales. He rebuilt the houses and had Carlton House built for himself. This was rebuilt in turn by John Nash, the King's favourite architect, in 1827. Stone from the older house was reused for the National Gallery in Trafalgar Square and an orangery at Kew Gardens.

Carmelite Street, EC4
On the opposite side of the river Fleet to the Black Friars, in the middle ages, were the monastic quarters of the Carmelite Order – the White Friars. Offices occupy the site of the order today.

Carter Lane, EC4
Two brothers, Stephen and Thomas Le Charetter (Carter), are shown as taxpayers in Castle Baynards Ward in 1319.

Carthusian Street, EC1
Sir Walter Manny founded a charterhouse, a monastic community, here in 1371 which became the London home of the Carthusian Order.

Cassland Road, E9
Sir John Cass, who bequeathed land and money to establish the Sir John Cass Institute, was a local resident.

Catherine Street, WC2
Towards the end of the seventeenth century there were a number of streets named after Charles II's wife, Catharine of Braganza. At one time during the early eighteenth century Pall Mall was shown as Catherine Street.

Cato Street, W1
Taking its name from a character in Roman history, Cato Street claimed the attention of the public in 1820, as the scene of an infamous conspiracy to assassinate Lord Castlereagh and other members of the Cabinet. With the help of a police spy named Edwards the plot was foiled and the premises were raided by police from Bow Street and by the Coldstream Guards. Arthur Thistlewood, the ringleader, and his fellow conspirators were found guilty of treason and hanged.

Cavendish Road, SW12
The famous chemist and philosopher Henry Cavendish set up his laboratories in Clapham, and here the weight of the earth was first calculated following his researches into the density of the planet.

Cavendish Street, Cavendish Square, W1
Lady Henrietta Cavendish Holles, who took her mother's maiden name, inherited the area on the death of her father.

Caxton Street, SW1
In the fifteenth century William Caxton, 'father of English printing', set up his presses under the shadow of nearby Westminster Abbey.

Chalk Farm Road, NW1
There is no direct connection with chalk or a farm here: the name is a corruption of the name of a large country house nearby, Chalcotts, at the end of England's Lane.

Chancery Lane, WC2
Early maps show the lane as New Lane, but it was later changed to Chancellor's or Chancery Lane following the setting up of the office of the Master of Rolls. Henry III (1207-72) had a house for converted Jews built here and this building later became the Rolls Office; today it is the Public Records Office.

Chandos Street, WC1
Charles Dickens knew this street when he worked at the blacking factory here. It was named after Lord Chandos in 1637, eighteen years before his death.

Change Alley, EC3
There are five ways in and out of Change Alley, fully titled (Royal) Exchange Alley from its proximity to the Exchange in Cornhill. Here until 1866 stood Garraway's Coffee House, the first place in the City to retail tea. Next door was Jonathan's Coffee House, where the Stock Exchange was started.

Chapel Street, NW1
When the chapel, loosely called Paddington Chapel, was first built in 1813 it was between Marylebone and Paddington and on the edge of the fields. It has since been replaced by offices.

Charing Cross, SW1
The statue of Charles I by Le Sueur stands at the end of Whitehall,

*The restored
Eleanor Cross
in the forecourt
of Charing
Cross station*

where the last of the Eleanor crosses was erected in 1291. The crosses were a memorial to Edward I's first wife, Eleanor of Castile, one being set up at each place the body of the queen rested on its journey from Harby in Nottinghamshire to Westminster Abbey for burial. The village of Charing stood on the bend of the river and took as its name the Saxon word for 'bend' – Charing.

Charing Cross Road, WC2

The road was created in 1887 as part of the plan for sweeping away the many alleys and slums of the area and making new arterial routes for the ever increasing traffic. The line of the road follows, roughly, that taken by the former Hog Lane, which was later called Crown Street.

Charles Street, W1

Lord Berkeley's brother Charles, Earl of Falmouth, is remembered in this street laid out *c.*1750.

27

Charles II Street, SW1
This street was built about 1671 and named after the monarch of the time.

Charterhouse Square, Charterhouse Street, Charterhouse Mews, EC1
In 1371 Sir Walter Manny bought land here and founded a charterhouse, or Carthusian monastery. It was established as a memorial to the thousands of victims of the Black Death of 1348 who are buried beneath the square.

Chatsworth Road, W4
Lord Hartington, later the fourth Duke of Devonshire, succeeded Richard Boyle to the title of Lord Burlington in 1753. The Chiswick estate of the Dukes of Devonshire was later administered from their Derbyshire house, Chatsworth.

Cheapside, EC2
Cheapside was the high street of the medieval City. With its many side streets it was a great open-air market, offering a wide variety of goods. Originally called after the Crown Inn which stood there, it was later named West Chepe (as opposed to East Chepe, which leads to the Tower of London) from the Saxon word for 'barter'. In addition to its market the street was also used for pageants, tournaments and other festivities.

Chelsea
Early charters refer to the place as *Celchyth*. which means a hithe (landing place) for chalk or lime. Alternatively, Norden reports a strand or riverside roadway, like a chesil, which 'the sea casteth up of sand and pebble stones'.

Chesham Place, SW1
Here was the seat of the Lowndes family. The name is taken from their country house at Chesham in Buckinghamshire.

Cheshire Court, EC4
The famous Ye Olde Cheshire Cheese tavern in Fleet Street attracts visitors and Londoners alike as it has done for over three hundred years.

Chesterfield Street, W1
Here stood the mansion, built in 1749, of the fourth Earl of

Chesterfield, who was described by Dr Johnson as 'a wit among lords and a lord among wits'. The Prince of Wales, later George IV, was a regular visitor to number 4, the home of Beau Brummell, who was teaching him how to tie a cravat.

Chester Square, SW1
The square is owned by the Dukes of Westminster, whose country estate is near the city of Chester.

Cheyne Walk, Cheyne Row, SW3 and SW10
Charles Cheyne was lord of the manor in the seventeenth century, but it was William, Lord Cheyne, who sold the area to Sir Hans Sloane in the early eighteenth century. Many famous people have been connected with Cheyne Walk, including George Eliot, who as Mrs Mary Cross died at her home here in 1890, Dante Gabriel Rossetti, and James McNeill Whistler. Thomas Carlyle lived in Cheyne Row for over forty-five years. His house is open to the public.

Chicheley Street, SE1
Henry Chichele, Archbishop of Canterbury in the fifteenth century, enlarged Lambeth Palace by adding the Lollards' Tower.

Chichester Rents, WC2
Bishop Ralph Nevill of Chichester built himself a town house here in 1228, during the reign of Henry III.

Chiswick
Anglo-Saxon charters show the village as *Ceswican*, which is translated as 'cheese farms'.

Chiswick Mall, W4
A mall is a pleasant riverside walk, and Chiswick Mall is no exception. Its domestic architecture ranges from the seventeenth to the twentieth centuries.

Chiswick Square, W4
The forecourt of Boston House forms an open square in front of the house which was first laid out in the seventeenth century. A notice on the wall records that here Becky Sharp, in Thackeray's *Vanity Fair*, threw out of the window of the coach the English dictionary she had been given as a leaving present from her school.

Weatherboarded cottage by Church Street, Chiswick

Christ Church Hill, NW3
Successor to the small chapel in Well Walk, Christ Church was built in 1852 to the designs of Sir Gilbert Scott, a local resident. It demonstrates the extent of residential development in the nineteenth century.

Church Entry, off Carter Lane, EC4
Leading from Carter Lane to Playhouse Yard, the alley marks the division between the nave and the choir of the Dominican priory (Black Friars) founded here in 1278.

Church Row, NW3
Architecturally one of the most attractive streets in London, with a variety of houses dating from the eighteenth century, it leads to the 'new' church of St John's, Hampstead.

Church Street
Every village had its parish church and the street leading up to it was almost inevitably named Church Street. As the metropolis grew and engulfed the surrounding villages, each Church Street added to its name that of the village to which it belonged.

Church Street, Chiswick, W4
In the old village of Chiswick, the west tower of the present parish church dates from the fifteenth century, while the rest of the church was rebuilt in the nineteenth century by John Loughborough Pearson. In the churchyard are the graves of Hogarth, Whistler and Kent and the cenotaph of Ugo Foscolo, the Italian patriot. Two of Oliver Cromwell's daughters are buried in unmarked graves within the church.

Clapham
Clapham is mentioned in the Domesday Survey of 1086 as *Clopeham*, *ham* meaning 'homestead' and *Clope* or *Cloppa* being the family name of the Saxon inhabitants, but the name has also been taken to mean 'the homestead on the hill'.

Clapham Park Road, SW4
The land was sold in 1824 to Thomas Cubitt, who laid out the estate of some 250 acres and turned it into a residential paradise – a parkland with streets laid out in pattern.

Clapham Road, SW9
It was formerly called Clapham Rise because of the slight gradient from Stockwell to the village of Clapham.

Clare Market, WC2
In this formerly residential area, John Holles's house, built in the seventeenth century, became Clare House when he was created Duke of Clare in Charles I's reign. After the restoration of the monarchy in 1660 the area became a centre for actors and many theatres and taverns were built here.

Clarence Terrace, NW1
Before he came to the throne in 1830, William IV was Duke of Clarence.

Clarges Street, W1
One of a number of mansions along Piccadilly, Clarges House was the home of General Monk's brother-in-law, Sir Charles Clarges. His son, Sir Walter, had this street laid out in 1717 on the ground adjoining the house.

Clement's Lane, EC4
First mentioned in 1309, the church dedicated to the patron saint of sailors was rebuilt by Wren after the Great Fire. It is the original church of the nursery rhyme 'Oranges and Lemons'; these fruits were unloaded on the riverside boundary of the parish.

Clerkenwell Green, EC1

The Worshipful Company of Parish Clerks of the City of London used to make a pilgrimage several times each year to the Clerks' Well, just outside the walls of the City. Here they performed their mystery plays, showing Bible stories in dramatic form.

Clerk's Place, EC2

Here in the thirteenth century stood the first hall of the Fraternity of St Nicholas – the Worshipful Company of Parish Clerks of the City of London. A City Corporation blue plaque marks the building which is now on the site of the company's hall.

Cleveland Row, SW1

It takes its name from the old Cleveland House and forms the south side of the square of the same name. Bridgewater House. designed by Sir Charles Barry in 1847, stands on the opposite side of the square.

Clifford's Inn, Fleet Street, EC4

Robert de Clifford was given the land here by Edward III and it remained in the family's possession until the fifteenth century. Since the previous century law students had rented the house for their studies. After the Great Fire, the commissioners appointed to assess losses and settle questions of property set up court here.

Clifford Street, W1

Named after Elizabeth Clifford, daughter of the last Earl of Cumberland, this was built on land belonging to the third Earl of Burlington. He had inherited the title of Lord Clifford and Baron Clifford of Lanesborough.

Clink Street, SE1

The Bishops of Winchester once owned this part of London and ruled over the area, which, being outside the jurisdiction of the City, became known as a Liberty. Within it was built a prison that became known as the Clink, probably from an old French word *clenche* or *clinque*, meaning a catch on the outside of a door.

Clissold Park, Clissold Crescent, N16

The Reverend Augustus Clissold, curate of St Mary's church, Stoke Newington, married the elder daughter of George Crawshay, a local landowner, on whose death the property passed to his daughter and son-in-law.

Cliveden Place, SW1
Cliveden House in Buckinghamshire was acquired in 1868 by the Grosvenor family, Dukes of Westminster, landlords of this site in London; in 1893 they sold Cliveden House to William Waldorf Astor.

Cloak Lane, EC4
This is probably a derivation of the Italian word for an open drain, *cloaco*. There was one here, leading down to the river Walbrook.

Cloth Fair, EC1
The principal cloth fair in England at the time of Elizabeth I was held in the churchyard of St Bartholomew the Great. Members of the Merchant Taylors' and Mercers' companies were present to ensure fair trading. Here, too, was set up a Piepowder Court (this name comes from the French for 'dusty feet') to administer the law to the wandering traders.

Cloudesley Square, Cloudesley Place, Cloudesley Road, Cloudesley Street, N1
Sir Richard Cloudesley died in 1517 and was buried in the churchyard of St Mary's, Islington. Although the church was bombed in the Second World War, his was one of the few tombs to survive. The church by Charles Barry in the centre of the square has been described as a brick version of King's College Chapel, Cambridge.

Coach and Horses Yard, W1
In the eighteenth century at the entrance to the mews here stood a public house, the Coach and Horses. It later changed to the Burlington Arms of today.

Cock Lane, EC1
At the junction of the lane with Giltspur Street is the place known as Pie Corner, one of the extremities of the Great Fire of 1666. High on the wall stands the gilded figure of a little naked boy, which was formerly part of the sign of a nearby tavern, the Fortune of War. Near here in the early middle ages was a pit for cock-fighting which is still remembered in the name of the lane.

Cockpit Steps, off Birdcage Walk, SW1
Cock-fighting was a popular pastime in the seventeenth and eighteenth centuries, but it has been banned in Britain for many years. A reconstructed pit can be seen at the Cockpit public house in St Andrew's Hill in the City. The pit off Birdcage Walk was demolished in 1816.

A Victorian engraving of the Great Fire of London (see Cock Lane)

Cockspur Street, SW1
Samuel Pepys records in his diary for 15th March 1669 how he and William Hewer visited the Cock Tavern at the end of Suffolk Street, linked by a spur to what is now Trafalgar Square.

Colebrooke Row, N1
Past owners of the manor of Highbury included the Colebrooke family.

Coleman Street, EC2
Authorities disagree as to the origin of this street's name. Some say that it is simply the name of the builder of the first house in the street, while others state that a man called Coleman built St Stephen's church, which once stood at one end of the street. It has also been suggested that charcoal burners (coal-men) set up their ovens here, but if so they may well have been soon told to move on, rather like the candlemakers of Candlewick Ward (see Cannon Street).

College Hill, EC4
Previously known as Paternoster Church Street, it was later re-

named after Sir Richard Whittington's college, set up here in the early fifteenth century.

College Road, NW10
This area is owned by Eton College, which has left its mark on the street names of the locality.

Compton Avenue, Compton Road, Compton Terrace, N1
The manor of Canonbury belonged to the Augustinian canons of St Bartholomew's, Smithfield. After the Dissolution it passed through the hands of a number of families, including the Comptons.

Conduit Street, W1
Taking its name from a conduit which brought water from the Tyburn river to a field known as Conduit Mead, the street was completed in 1713.

Connaught Place, Connaught Street, Connaught Square, W2
Houses that have long since been demolished are remembered in the street names of today. Originally, when Prince Frederick, Duke of Gloucester and Edinburgh, lived here, it was called Edinburgh Place, but this was later changed to Connaught after the Duke's secondary title. In 1813 the Prince Regent's unhappy wife, Caroline, moved here.

Cons Street, SE1
Emma Cons was the founder of the Royal Victoria Coffee Music Hall, which later became the Old Vic Theatre.

Constitution Hill, SW1
Strype, the London historian, describes the roadway as the 'road to Kensington'. The reason for the present name is obscure but it could be that it was where kings took their constitutional walk at the time that the land belonged to nearby St James's Palace.

Cooper's Row, EC3
On the wall at the end of the row is a painting showing it as it was in the middle ages when it was known as Woodruffe Lane from the surname of the owner of the land, which in turn is derived from an English woodland flower. The street was renamed in 1750 when the coopers (barrel-makers) were predominant in this area.

Copenhagen Street, N1
It is uncertain whether it is named after a pleasure resort here in 1752 or from an inn set up in the previous century for the particular use of the Danish community of London.

Eighteenth-century Cornhill and Lombard Street

Coram's Fields, WC1

Thomas Coram, a sea captain, was so horrified at the number of foundling children he saw on the streets of London that he set up here the Foundling Hospital – or, to give it its full name, the Hospital for the Maintenance and Education of Exposed and Deserted Children.

Cork Street, W1

This street is another reminder of the title of Richard, Earl of Burlington and Cork, and his ownership of property here.

Cornhill, EC3

Two possible origins of this street's name are given by historians. The first is that here was a hill of the City on which corn was grown and that it later developed into a market; the second, that it is derived from the ownership of the land here in the twelfth century by the family called Cornhell or Hupcornehill. The original street stretched from Aldgate Pump to the site of the present road junction at the Bank. At the junction of Cornhill, Bishopsgate, Leadenhall Street and Gracechurch Street stood the standard from which distances to the City were measured.

Covent Garden, WC2
Monks of Westminster Abbey kept a kitchen garden here from which they sold surplus produce to the local population. At the dissolution of the monasteries in the sixteenth century the land was granted to the Protector Somerset, and on his fall from power to John Russell, the first Earl of Bedford. In 1631 the fourth Earl commissioned Inigo Jones to lay out the square and the surrounding streets. Jones designed an Italian piazza and, on its west side, the parish church of St Paul, once described as the 'handsomest barn in England'. It is also known as the actors' church because of its many theatrical associations. In front of the church, on the square side, parliamentary elections took place, as well as the first 'Punch and Judy' show in England, which was witnessed by Samuel Pepys, as he records in his diary.

Coventry Street, W1
When Henry Coventry, Secretary of State to Charles II, bought a house here in the 1670s he renamed it Coventry House. The street was later called Coventry in his honour.

Cowcross Street, EC1
Here the cows are supposed to have crossed on their way to the slaughterhouses and Smithfield market.

Cowley Street, SW1
This street was named after a country house at Cowley, in the old county of Middlesex, owned by a famous eighteenth-century actor named Barton Booth. His rise to fame and wealth began in 1713 with his celebrated performance as Cato in Joseph Addison's play of the same name.

Cowper's Court, EC3
In the reign of James I Sir William Cowper set up a large house here in the City.

Cox's Walk, SE21
Leading from the side of St Peter's Church, Lordship Lane, the Walk takes its name either from David Cox, the painter, who lived near Dulwich Ponds, or from Francis Cox, tenant of the Green Man, who had the privilege of cutting a walk through the woods here.

Craig's Court, Whitehall, SW1
Hiding behind the more modern buildings of Whitehall, the court is named after Secretary Craggs's father, the friend of Pope and Addison. One side is dominated by Harrington House, until 1917 the town residence of the Earls of Harrington. Built at the turn of the eighteenth

century, today it houses the offices of Whitehall telephone exchange.

Cramer Street, W1
Wilhelm Cramer, the German violinist, lived and died in London in the eighteenth century.

Cranbourn Street, WC2
This was named from a secondary title of the Earls of Salisbury, whose house was nearby, off the present-day St Martin's Lane.

Crane Avenue, W3
A. C. Crane was a member of the Acton Urban District Council at the time of George V's Coronation in 1910.

Crane Court, off Fleet Street, EC4
Though much altered in recent years, it takes its name from the Two-Crane Inn which formerly stood at its entrance. The Royal Society was founded here in the seventeenth century.

Craven Hill Gardens, W2
Houses built on the land of the Earls of Craven have a stipulation in the lease that, should the land be required for the building of a pest house then it must be used for that purpose. Pest houses date from the seventeenth century when areas outside the bounds of the City were used to provide places of refuge in time of plague.

Craven Street, WC2
Though known as Spur Alley in 1742, its present title derives from the landowners of the previous century, the Earls of Craven.

Crawford Passage, EC1
This was once called Pickled Egg Walk from the reputation of the principal tavern for these delicacies. Tradition says that Charles I, passing close by, stopped and partook of a pickled egg. The passage was renamed after Peter Crawford, the owner of the tavern in the eighteenth century.

Creechurch Lane, EC3
Originally a small lane or passageway running beside the wall of Aldgate Priory, Holy Trinity, whose alternative title is Christ Church. Over the years the name became corrupted from Christ to Cree Church.

Creed Lane, EC4
Processions were commonplace in medieval London and especially so around St Paul's Cathedral. When the rosary was chanted round the streets, the *Credo*, the creed or public statement of faith,

was spoken at this point.

Crescent Grove, SW4
An attractive piece of early nineteenth-century town planning, this forms a crescent.

Crooms Hill, SE10
The name comes from the Old English word for crooked, *crom.* The hill is steep and winding.

Crosby Square, off Bishopsgate, EC3
Until 1907, when it was taken down and rebuilt on the Chelsea Embankment, where it still survives, Crosby Hall stood here. The home of Sir John Crosby, the hall was built in 1470. At one time it was owned and lived in by Sir Thomas More.

Crosswall, EC3
Known as John Street, after King John, following an Act of Parliament of 1760 'for the opening of streets to be made in the City of London', it has also been shown on maps as Horseshoe Alley. Early in the twentieth century it was given a new name which denotes its position across the line of the city wall.

Crown Court, WC2
It was in the Crown Tavern here that the magazine *Punch* was first projected.

Crown Office Row, Temple, EC4
Charles Lamb was born at number 2 in 1775; there is a stone plaque on the modern

Crown Office Row

building on the site. The row is so called after the Crown Office.

Crown Passage, off Pall Mall, SW1
One of the few survivors of the many quaint courts of the area built in Georgian days is opposite St James's Palace with all its royal connections.

Croxted Road, SE21 and SE24
A winding, twisting and turning road shown in 1334 as Croketret, with large trees, hedgerows and ditches, it formed part of the pilgrims' route from the ferries of Lambeth to Canterbury.

Cruden Street, N1
The compiler of one of the best-known concordances of the Bible, Alexander Cruden, died in a house in Islington.

Crutched Friars, EC3
An Augustinian order, the Friars of the Holy Cross, was founded here in 1298 by Ralph Hosiar and William Sabernes. Their dress was a blue habit on which was superimposed, both back and front, a red cross made out of leather, and soon they became known as the crossed or crutched friars.

Cullum Street, EC3
The street linking Fenchurch Street and Lime Street is shown by Stow as Culver Alley, without any explanation. But 'culver' is an ancient name for a pigeon, a bird that has long been at home in the City. Sir John Cullum, sheriff in 1646, gave the altar steps of nearby St Dynios Backchurch. The church was demolished in the nineteenth century, but the street recalls his name.

Cursitor Street, EC4
The officials who issued writs in the Court of Chancery were called in Latin *clerici de cursa*. There were twenty-four of them and they were never very popular people. They no longer have a place in the justices' work but the name survives in the street.

Curzon Street, W1
This was named after the third Earl Howe, George Augustus Curzon, although early maps of the area show it as Mayfair Row. In Thackeray's *Vanity Fair* Mr and Mrs Rawdon Crawley live in this street.

Cutler Street, E1
Land was left here to the Cutlers' Company in 1469 by one Agnes Carter. At that time it was an inn called the Woolsack. In *c.*1730 the Company developed the property with warehouses and

tenements and created Cutler Street.

Dacre Street, SW1
This was named after a Lord Dacre who owned property here.

Danvers Street, SW3
Leading from the Chelsea Embankment, the street was once the way to the riverside house of Sir John Danvers, one of the signatories of Charles I's death warrant.

D'Arblay Street, W1
In the mid eighteenth century the writer and novelist Frances Burney, later Madame D'Arblay, spent the early part of her life here with her father, Dr Charles Burney, the composer and music historian.

Darnley Road, E9
Lord Darnley, husband of Mary, Queen of Scots, lived in his youth at Barber's Barn with his mother, the Lady Margaret Douglas, Countess of Lennox.

Dartmouth Street, SW1
This street is called after an Earl of Dartmouth who lived in a house in Queen Square (now part of Queen Anne's Gate).

Davies Street, W1
Mary Davies, daughter of Alexander Davies, married Sir Thomas Grosvenor and it was through this union that most of the property in the vicinity came into the possession of the Grosvenor family.

Deanery Street, W1
The Dean and Chapter of Westminster Abbey, landlords of the ground, first called this Dean and Chapter Street in 1737.

Dean's Court, EC4
Halfway down one side, set back slightly from the roadway, was the official residence of the Dean of St Paul's Cathedral – hence Dean's Court. The Dean now lives in Amen Court.

Dean Street, W1
As Bishop of London, Henry Compton also acted as the Dean of the Chapel Royal at the time when this street was being developed. The eighteenth-century actress Peg Woffington lived in the street.

Westminster Abbey viewed from Dean's Yard

Dean's Yard, SW1

Providing a pleasant green oasis for visitors to stroll through and the boys of Westminster School to play on, the yard is within the jurisdiction of the Dean and Canons of Westminster Abbey.

De Beauvoir Crescent, De Beauvoir Road, De Beauvoir Square, N1

Born in Guernsey in the Channel Islands, Richard de Beauvoir bought land here in 1680.

Defoe Road, N16

In the anteroom of the public library in Church Street, Stoke Newington, is a marble bust of Daniel Defoe, one of the former borough's most distinguished residents.

Denmark Hill, SE5

Once shown as Dulwich Hill, it was later renamed in honour of Prince George of Denmark, Queen Anne's husband, who lived here.

Denmark Street, WC2
The 'Tin Pan Alley' of London's music-publishing industry, it was also named after Prince George of Denmark.

Derby Gate, off Whitehall, SW1
On the corner is the Red Lion public house, mentioned by Charles Dickens in *David Copperfield*. Previously the site had been occupied by a town house of the Earls of Derby, but it was surrendered to Parliament in the seventeenth century.

De Vere Gardens, W8
On the death of Geoffrey, Bishop of Coutances, in 1093, the area of Kensington came into the ownership of the De Vere family, who came from Ver, near Bayeux in Normandy. They were one of the families who helped William, Duke of Normandy, in his conquest of England.

Devereux Court, WC2
High on the outside wall of the Devereux Arms hotel is the bust of Robert Devereux, Earl of Essex, who died in 1676. Beneath the bust is the inscription: 'This is Devereux Court 1676'.

Devonshire Gardens, W4
The daughter of Richard Boyle, Earl of Burlington, married into the Devonshire family and on the death of her father inherited the Chiswick estate.

Devonshire Row, Devonshire Square, EC2
During the seventeenth century the Cavendish family, Earls of Devonshire, had a house here in Bishopsgate.

Dorrington Street, EC1
Sometimes spelt without the 'g', the street was built by Thomas Dorrington, a citizen and bricklayer of London.

Dorset Rise, EC4
The Dorset Garden Theatre opened here in 1676.

Dorset Square, NW1
North of the Portman estate in Marylebone, the square was developed in the nineteenth century by the Earls of Dorset and was first laid out in 1819.

Doughty Street, WC1
Charles Dickens, who lived at number 48, used the name Brownlow

for a character in *Oliver Twist*. The Brownlows were the direct heirs of the Doughty family, which once owned land here.

Dover Street, W1
On land granted to him by Charles II, Henry Jermyn, Earl of Dover, built the street in 1686.

Dowgate Hill, EC4
The final course of the Walbrook river leads to Dow Gate, which is said to have derived from Duna, the old English name of the owner of the gate, hithe or dock on the riverbank here.

Downing Street, SW1
A blind alley, originally built *c*.1680 by Sir George Downing, ambassador at The Hague under both the Commonwealth and Charles II, its construction was an act of housing speculation typical of the seventeenth century. It is ironic that a man described as a rogue should be commemorated in such a celebrated street.

Drury Lane, WC2
So called from the Druries family, who lived in a house here in the sixteenth century. In the following century the house was rebuilt by Lord Craven and named Craven House.

Duchess of Bedford's Walk, W8
A lodge for the Dowager Duchess of Bedford was built near here.

Duke of York Steps, SW1
Every child knows of the Grand Old Duke of York who had ten thousand

Duke of York Steps

men and how he marched them up and down the hill. His commemorative column, 124 feet high, stands at the head of the steps and his statue looks down on people walking up and down them daily. The son of George III, the Duke was Commander-in-chief of the British Army from 1798 to 1828. By nature a very extravagant man, he died leaving dozens of unpaid bills. The column is said to have been erected by 'voluntary' contribution from the members of the army at the time, but in fact each man had a day's pay stopped, from the newest recruit to the longest-serving field marshal.

Duke of York Street, SW1
This is named as a compliment to the Duke of York, later James II, whose brother, Charles II, is also remembered locally.

Duke's Place, EC3
By his marriage to Sir Thomas Audley's daughter, Thomas Howard, Duke of Norfolk, gained possession of the precincts of the priory of Holy Trinity, Aldgate.

Duke Street, W1
The name is derived from Frederick Augustus (second son of George III), the Duke of York and Albany, 'the Grand Old Duke of York'. He also gave his name to The Albany on the opposite side of Piccadilly after he purchased it from the first Lord Melbourne.

Dulwich College Road, SE21
The lord of the manor, Edward Alleyn, an actor and contemporary of Shakespeare, founded the 'College of God's Gift' in 1605. Today the school has become Dulwich College.

Duncannon Street, WC2
With the development of the Charing Cross area and the laying out of Trafalgar Square in the early nineteenth century new streets came into being. In 1837 the Chief Commissioner of Woods and Forests was Lord Duncannon.

Eastcheap, EC3
This was the eastern market of the medieval city of London. 'East' distinguishes it from its counterpart in another place.

Eaton Square, SW1
The seat of the Dukes of Westminster in Cheshire was Eaton Hall

Prime Minister Stanley Baldwin's house in Eaton Square.

and they were the landowners when the square was being built.

Ebury Street, Ebury Bridge, Ebury Square, SW1
At the time of Elizabeth I there was a farm here known as Eubery Farm, covering some 430 acres. The name is derived from the Saxon words *ey* (water) and *burgh* (a fortified place) and is mentioned in a grant by Edward I.

Eccleston Street, Eccleston Square, SW1
The ground landlords of Belgravia, the Dukes of Westminster, had a mansion, Eaton Hall, near the village of Eccleston in Cheshire.

Edensor Road, W4
The village of Edensor, near Chatsworth, the estate of the Dukes of Devonshire, was rebuilt in the nineteenth century in order to improve the view from the house.

Edgware Road, NW2, NW9, W2
This road follows the course of Watling Street, the Roman road that leads from Marble Arch to the former Middlesex village of Edgware, on its way from Dover to Chester.

Effra Road, SW2 and SW19
The Effra river was one of the larger rivers of the London area, but it now flows underground, like so many others. Its source is in the hills of Norwood and it flows through Brixton, along the south side of the Oval and enters the Thames near Vauxhall Bridge. In Elizabethan times it was navigable at least to Brixton. John Ruskin

(1819-1900) recalls that when he was barely thirteen years old he drew the bridge over the river near Herne Hill station: 'This sketch was the first in which I was ever supposed to show any talent for drawing.'

Electric Avenue, SW9
When the avenue, with its shopping arcade, was opened in the 1880s it became the first street in London lit by electricity. This extended the shopping day.

Elm Row, NW3
Off Heath Street, Hampstead, the row of early eighteenth-century cottages replaces the elm trees of earlier times.

Ely Court, EC1
The only habitable building in the court, which links Hatton Garden with Ely Place, is the Mitre Tavern, whose sign is the three-sided hat of the Bishops of Ely on whose land the house stands.

Ely Place, EC1
Here stood the palace of the Bishops of Ely until Elizabeth I forced Bishop Cox to give his property here to her favourite, Sir Christopher Hatton.

Essex Road, N1
Robert Devereux, Earl of Essex, had a country house here in the sixteenth century where he often entertained Elizabeth I. The Old Queen's Head public house is said to be on the site of the house.

Essex Street, WC2
First laid out in 1673 by Dr Nicholas Barbon, Essex Street took its name from the former favourite of Elizabeth I, Robert Devereux, Earl of Essex, whose house stood here on the banks of the river. It has long since disappeared but the staircase from it can be seen in number 24, while at the end of the street is the watergate which once led into the grounds of the house from the river. The good doctor was known as Barebones to his contemporaries and was the son of 'Praisegod' Barebones, MP for the City of London in 1653 and fierce opponent of the restoration of Charles II.

Eton Road, NW3
This is built on land owned by Eton College, the famous public school near Windsor, which was founded by Henry VI in 1440 when he was only twenty years old.

Farm Street, Mayfair

Exeter Street, WC2
Exeter House was one of the numerous mansions that once lined the Strand. It was built for the Earl of Exeter, the eldest son of Lord Burleigh, one of Elizabeth I's statesmen.

Exhibition Road, SW7
One of the great achievements of the nineteenth century was the Great Exhibition held in 1851 in Hyde Park.

Fair Street, SE1
This was the site of the once famous Horseley Down Fair, and was named after it.

Falconberg Mews, W1
In the seventeenth century the Earl of Falconberg set up his town house here and brought his second wife, Mary, the daughter of Oliver Cromwell, to live in it.

Falcon Court, EC4
Here was the office of Wynkyn de Worde, the early printer, friend and later successor of William Caxton, the 'father of English printing', whose sign was the falcon.

Farm Street, W1
It is difficult to imagine any connection between agriculture and this fashionable street, but before the development of the district in the eighteenth century there was indeed a large farmhouse near where the street is today.

Farringdon Street, EC4
The street is new in formation, having been first laid out in 1826. Its name and that of its extension beyond the City's boundaries, Farringdon Road, derived from William de Farndon, an alderman and sheriff in 1282.

Fellows Road, NW3
The Provost and Fellows of Eton College, landowners in the vicinity, developed the area by building houses and a church.

Fenchurch Street, Fenchurch Avenue, EC3
This street close by the haymarket derives its title from the Latin *faenum* (hay), but the church of St Gabriel (see Fen Court) was said to have been built on fenny or marshy land.

Fen Court, EC3
All that remains of the church of St Gabriel Fenchurch is a garden laid out in the former churchyard.

Fentiman Road, SW8
Near Kennington Oval, in the eighteenth century Mr Fentiman bought several acres of marshland which he converted into a plantation and a pleasure ground with a mansion for himself.

Fetter Lane, EC4
Here gathered idlers and the unemployed, and from the word 'fewters', meaning beggars, the present name has evolved. Public executions frequently took place at either end of the lane. For his part in the poet Waller's conspiracy to seize the City for Charles I, Nathaniel Tomkins was executed on 5th July 1643 at the Holborn end of the lane. Ben Jonson seems to have thought that the place was a rival of Lombard Street with its moneylenders. He makes Fungoso, in *Every Man out of his Humour*, say that he 'can borrow forty shillings on his gown in Fetter Lane'. An alternative derivation is from the felt-makers or 'feuriers' who lived here at some time in the past.

Finch Lane, EC3
Sir Robert Finke was an early benefactor of the local church of St

49

Benet (Benedict), which was destroyed in 1842 to make way for the new Royal Exchange designed by Sir William Tite (1798-1873).

Finsbury Pavement, EC2
This was once the only firm path across the marshy area of Moorfields.

Fishmongers Hall Street, EC4
Since the time of Edward III in the fourteenth century the Worshipful Company of Fishmongers has had its hall here by the river Thames.

Fish Street Hill, EC3
This leads from the pathway of the medieval London Bridge to Billingsgate market, first established for the sale of fish in 1699.

Fitzmaurice Place, W1
This comes from the family name of the Marquis of Lansdowne, who owned land here.

Fitzroy Square, W1
Grandson of Charles II and son of the first Duke of Grafton, the Honourable Charles Fitzroy was Lord of Tottenhall.

Fleet Street during the Lord Mayor's Show

Flask Walk, NW3
Spas and wells abounded around London in the seventeenth and eighteenth centuries, and their patrons often took the waters back to their homes in flasks. One of the oldest beerhouses in Hampstead, whose sign shows a soldier with his gunpowder flask, stands in the walk.

Fleet Road, NW3
One of London's 'lost' rivers, long since channelled underground for most of its course from Hampstead Heath, the Fleet enters the Thames at Blackfriars.

Fleet Street, EC4
In its journey from its source in Hampstead the river Fleet is referred to by several different names, from the Kent or Cant to the Oldebourne. A roadway directly connecting the Strand to Ludgate, Fleetbridge Street, to use its original name, crossed the river Fleet at what is now Ludgate Circus. In the nineteenth century excavations uncovered the arch spring of the bridge built over the river by Sir Christopher Wren. The name is derived from the Anglo-Saxon word for a tidal inlet that had sufficient water to float boats. Strictly speaking, therefore, the name should be applied only to the lower reaches of the river.

Fleetwood Street, N16
Charles Fleetwood, the third son of Sir Miles Fleetwood, and a distinguished Cromwellian soldier, took part in the trial of Charles I but his only punishment at the Restoration of the monarchy in 1660 was to be declared 'perpetually incapacitated from all offices of trust'. Fleetwood House, built by Sir Edward Hartopp, contained over fifty rooms and stood in eight acres of ground.

Foster Lane, EC2
Passing through the forms Vastes, Fastes, Faster, Fauster and finally Foster, the word originates from the title of the church at one end of the lane – St Vedast, the sixth-century saint and Bishop of Arras in France.

Foubert's Place, W1
This was named after a Frenchman who ran a riding school here during the reign of Charles II.

Founderers Court, EC2
Brassfounders set up their hall here during the middle ages. It later became a hotbed of sedition at the time of the French Revolution.

Fountain Court, Temple, EC4
Ruth Pinch met John Westbrook here, by the fountain in the centre of the court, in Charles Dickens's novel *Martin Chuzzlewit*. The fountain still plays today, surrounded by mulberry trees.

Fowler Road, N1
This was named after the family of Sir Thomas Fowler, who entertained Elizabeth I here during the sixteenth century.

Frampton Park Road, E9
Although he had only one arm, Major Heathfield Frampton served with honour in the Crimean War and, when captured by the Russians, won their respect. He was taken to St Petersburg and 'treated with much kindness by the Tsar and his family'. His connection with the old borough of Hackney is that he lived here for a short time.

Frederick's Place, EC2
The place is named from the Frederick family whose mansion stood here in the seventeenth century. One member, Sir John Frederick, became Lord Mayor of London in 1662.

French Ordinary Court, EC3
Here could be bought an 'ordinary' French meal at a fixed sum.

Friary Court, St James's Palace, SW1
When Charles II married Catharine of Braganza she brought in her retinue a group of friars who set up their quarters in the palace here.

Friday Street, EC4
Found in the twelfth century as 'Fridei Strete', it is said to owe its name to the fishmongers who held Friday markets here to sell fish to the citizens, who ate fish on Fridays in memory of Good Friday. There are a number of hamlets in England called Friday Street, one of the most beautiful being in Surrey. But they cannot have all been used just to sell fish!

Frith Street, W1
In St James's Square stood St Albans House, built for Henry Jermyn, Earl of St Albans, by James Frith, the architect, who is remembered in this street in the Soho district of London.

Furnival Street, EC4
Sir William Furnival owned land here on which was built an inn of Chancery, Furnival Inn. Charles Dickens lived here for a time.

The new Garrick Club, engraved in 1864

Gallery Road, SE21
Dulwich Picture Gallery was built to the designs of Sir John Soane in 1814. It was founded by Noel and Margaret Desenfans, who are buried in sarcophagi in the museum. The gallery was the first public art gallery in London.

Garlick Hill, EC4
Garlic was unloaded on the hithe at the riverside and sold on the hillside near the church of St James.

Garrick Street, WC2
Not far from the Drury Lane Theatre that he managed, David Garrick, the actor-manager, is commemorated here in the names of both the street and the Garrick Club.

Gate Street, WC2
When Lincoln's Inn Fields were first laid out in the early seventeenth century the area was enclosed in order to prevent undesirable characters from entering. Gates, suitably guarded, were installed to enable the residents to enter or leave.

Gauden Road, SW4

Sir Dennis Gauden, brother of the Bishop of Exeter and Master of the Temple, built a large house on the north side of Clapham Common in the seventeenth century. The estate around the house was later bought by William Hewer, the partner and friend of Samuel Pepys, the diarist.

Gayfere Street, SW1

The street was named after a churchwarden of St John's, Smith Square, and master mason of Westminster Abbey, who died here in 1812.

George Street, W1

Containing the famous church of St George, Hanover Square, and originally called Great George Street, it was so named in honour of George I in 1719.

George Yard, off Lombard Street, EC3

Records show that an ordinary house here was converted into an alehouse in the twelfth century and later became the George. After the Great Fire of 1666 it was joined with the nearby Living Vulture and the coaching yard became a public square. The London lodging house of the Earl of Ferrers stood on the corner of the yard in the twelfth century and when his brother was murdered the body was thrown on to the street. As a direct result of this deed a night watch was set up.

Gerrard Street, W1

In the seventeenth century, after the end of the Civil War, the Earl of Macclesfield, whose family name was Gerrard, set up a walled exercise ground, the Military Yard, to the south of where Shaftesbury Avenue now runs. The street first appears on maps in the early eighteenth century.

Gibson Square, N1

Designed by Thomas Cubitt and first occupied in 1832, the square's name commemorates the ground landlord, Thomas Milber Gibson, member of parliament for Ipswich.

Giltspur Street, EC1

Leading to Smithfield, the City's great arena for tournaments and other public displays, the name of the street is a reminder of the spurs to be won there, and perhaps sold here too.

Gipsy Hill, SE19
The hill was so called from the large encampments of gipsies that were frequently to be found here.

Gloucester Road, SW7
George Canning, Prime Minister for a hundred days in 1827, moved into Gloucester Lodge, the name of which was changed from Orford House to honour a widowed Duchess of Gloucester.

Godliman Street, EC4
Godelmynnes were a kind of cordwain (shoe) made from the skin of a young animal; the name apparently derives from the town of Godalming in Surrey, where the trade of tanning flourished. Cordwainery, the art of shoemaking, is so called after Cordoba in Spain. The Cordwainers Hall stood not far from this street.

Golden Square, W1
A builder called Golding first laid out the square in the seventeenth century and its name later became shortened to Golden Square.

Goswell Road, EC1
Many wells around the City had their own tracks or roadways leading to them. This one led to Godes-well.

Gough Square, EC4
Archive documents indicate that the square was named after Sir Richard Gough, but that a certain Nicholas Gough, a master printer by trade, also set up business here in the eighteenth century. Printing and publishing have been centred in the area from these times.

Gracechurch Street, EC3
The street is named from the closeness of a church, St Benet's, to the grass (hay) market in Fenchurch Street.

Grafton Street, W1
Further speculation in building the new West End of London in the eighteenth century led the Duke of Grafton to buy land in this part and to have a house built here. It was known previously as 'Ducking Pond Row' and may have had a pond and ducking stool for punishing women.

Grandison Road, SW11
Oliver St John, Viscount Grandison, bought the manor here from Charles I.

Gray's Inn Road, WC1
In 1314 John de Gray gave land here to St Bartholomew's Priory in order that masses might be said for the repose of his soul. Later the inn was let to law students and their tutors.

Great College Street, SW1
Abbot Litlington built a wall around the garden of Westminster Abbey in 1363. On the other side of the roadway is a pleasant row of eighteenth-century houses.

Great Scotland Yard, SW1
Famous as one of the original offices of the Metropolitan Police Force, and more recently as the Army Recruiting Office, here was the royal house where kings of Scotland stayed when visiting English monarchs. Later, after the unification of the two kingdoms of England and Scotland with the accession of King James VI of Scotland as James I of England, the palace was used by the royal architects, including in their time Inigo Jones, Christopher Wren and John Vanbrugh.

Great Smith Street, SW1
The names of landowners are often recorded in the street names on their estates and here Sir James Smith was the ground owner and developer in the eighteenth century.

Great Titchfield Street, W1
The Dukes of Portland, local landowners, have the secondary title of Marquess of Titchfield.

Great Tower Street, EC3
This is an obvious choice of title for a street so close to the Tower of London and leading directly to it.

Great Trinity Lane, EC4
Stow records in 1598 that the church of Holy Trinity here was very old and in danger of falling down. It was not rebuilt after the Great Fire.

Great Windmill Street, W1
In the seventeenth century a windmill stood in nearby Haymarket. Its site later became Shaver's Hall, a gaming house.

Greek Street, W1
At the south-east corner of Soho Square, the street was laid out in 1680 and contained a Greek church that was attended by the local Greek community.

Gresham Street and the church of St Lawrence

Greencoat Place, SW1
Charity schools were plentiful in the eighteenth century, and their pupils wore coats of distinctive colour.

Green Street, W1
This was simply a plot of land covered with grass, between Park Lane and Oxford Street, when the street was first designed.

Greenwich
This medieval fishing village whose name means 'green village', from the Saxon, later became famous for its royal palace of Placenta or Bella (beautiful) Court.

Gresham Street, EC2
Until 1815 maps show the street as Lad Lane from Milk Street to Wood Street, and as Cateaton Street from Old Jewry to Milk Street. Its further extension was known as St Ann's Lane and this did not change its name until 1877. Gresham is the name of a family remembered in the City for its benevolence in establishing a college 'where free lectures were to be given to all who care to attend', a Royal Exchange that was to confirm the Venerable Bede's statement that the City is 'a mart of many nations', and a bank that has since been merged with Martin's Bank.

Greville Street, EC1
Fulke Greville, Lord Brooke, an Elizabethan courtier, built a mansion here in the sixteenth century.

Greycoat Place, SW1
The Royal Foundation of Queen Anne, in the parish of St Margaret, Westminster, and commonly called the Grey Coat Hospital, was founded in 1698 by eight worthy citizens of Westminster. Originally sited in Broad Sanctuary, the Hospital moved to its present situation in the early eighteenth century, and it is from its early days of occupying land owned by Westminster Abbey that the school has built up strong connections with the abbey. In 1874 the Hospital became a Church of England grammar school for girls; it is now a comprehensive school.

Grosvenor Crescent, SW1
The crescent occupies the area known as Five Fields, which was bare and swampy until 1825 when, by special Act of Parliament, Lord Grosvenor developed the estate. The crescent was laid out between 1837 and 1860. St George's Hospital stood at one end of the street, where Tattersall's horse market was before its move to Knightsbridge Green.

Grosvenor Square, W1
After Lincoln's Inn Fields, this is the largest of London's fashionable squares; it covers about six acres and was first laid out in 1695 by William Kent for Sir Richard Grosvenor.

Grosvenor Street, W1
A later development than the square, but part of the same design, it was formed about 1726.

The Grove, NW5
A long shady avenue, for the most part tree-lined, it has interesting houses on either side of the roadway.

Gun Street, E1
In his *Survay* [sic] *of London* of 1598 John Stow the historian refers to this area as 'whereunto the gunners of the Tower do weekly repair...'. The street is on the site of the artillery ground.

Gutter Lane, EC2
As early as 1180 the lane is shown as 'Godrun', which could have been the first name of a woman. Or, might not this have been one of the few streets of the City to have a gutter to help the garbage on its way?

Ha-Ha Road, SE18
A device much used in the landscape garden designs of the eighteenth century, a ha-ha has been described as 'an invisible fence or hedge'. Charles Bridgeman first introduced it to Great Britain, taking the idea from a French gardening book, *La Theorie et la pratique du jardinage*, published anonymously in France in 1703, and translated into English by John James in 1712.

Half Moon Street, W1
One of the numerous taverns of Piccadilly stood here and its sign was a half moon. The street was built *c.*1730 and the house on its corner was the last one in Piccadilly to use brick, all the others being made of stone.

Halkin Street, SW1
The Dukes of Westminster had a seat at Halkin Castle in Clwyd. Originally the street terminated at the mud banks of Five Fields, a marsh-like expanse of ground.

Halton Place, Halton Road, N1
Van Dyck painted the portrait of the handsome Cavalier Sir William Halton, who was the local landowner at the time of the Civil War.

Hamilton Place, W1
During the reign of Charles II, the Ranger of Hyde Park, Colonel James Hamilton, built a short cul-de-sac which was later joined to Park Lane.

Hampstead
First mentioned in a charter of King Edgar in 957, the village is a 'homestead' or 'farm'.

Hampstead Square, NW3
A square only in name, it has one or two old houses and is part of the new Hampstead of the seventeenth and eighteenth centuries.

Hanover Square, W1
Through his marriage to Lady Henrietta Holles in 1713 the second Earl of Oxford came into ownership of the land north and south of Oxford Street. It was intended to call the square Oxford after his earldom but as a loyal afterthought it was named in honour of the monarch George I's homeland.

Hans Place, SW1
This derives from the Christian name of Sir Hans Sloane, one of

Chelsea's most noted inhabitants, a physician and collector whose collections became, after his death, the basis of the British Museum.

Hanway Street, Hanway Place, W1
Jonas Hanway was the first gentleman to carry an umbrella through the streets of London. He was buried at Hampton Court and has a memorial in Westminster Abbey. He was a Governor of the Foundling Hospital in Holborn and was noted for his tireless devotion to the plight of deserted children in eighteenth-century London. He was described by Horace Walpole as 'one of the apostles of humanity'.

Harcourt Street, W1
John Harcourt bought property in the vicinity and made his home here.

Hare Court, The Temple, EC4
Nicholas Hare, Master of the Rolls, died here in 1557. Thackeray had chambers at number 1 in 1831.

Harley Street, W1
Edward Harley, owing his title of Lord Harley to his father, the great statesman, married into the Cavendish Holles family and in the 1720s developed the land here that came with his wife.

Harp Lane, EC3
Until quite recently houses and shops did not have numbers for identification purposes; instead signs were used, hung from the buildings. Here was a messuage (a dwelling house with outbuildings and surrounding grounds) whose sign was *le harpe*. The Worshipful Company of Bakers of the City of London has its hall on the site today.

Harrow Road, W2
Long before the Romans built their splendid roads through Britain, the countryside was criss-crossed with ancient tracks and bridleways. Some of these narrow ways remain today, and this is one of them, leading to the former village of Harrow-on-the-Hill.

Hatton Garden, EC1
Sir Christopher Hatton, a favourite of Elizabeth I, coveted the house and gardens of the Bishops of Ely at Holborn. At first the Bishop, Richard Cox, refused to release the property to the Lord Chancellor but after receiving a stern letter of rebuke from the Queen herself that threatened to unfrock him if he did not comply

Sir Christopher Hatton

with her wishes, he moved to other living quarters. For his trouble the prelate was paid ten pounds, ten loads of hay and a red rose each year. Shakespeare in *Richard III* has the Duke of Gloucester ask the Bishop for some of the excellent strawberries that he had seen in the gardens of the palace. All that is visible today of the palace buildings is the chapel now used by Roman Catholics and dedicated to St Etheldreda.

Haverstock Hill, NW3
Cattle are said to have grazed on the hill in former times. The Low Latin word for cattle is *averia*, hence *aver*, and *haver* when anglicised.

Hay Hill, W1
Hay Hill Farm stood on the banks of the river Tyburn's tributary,

the Aye or Eye brook, which still runs underground at the foot of the hill into Berkeley Street. George IV, while still Prince of Wales, was once waylaid by some footpads here who robbed him and some friends of two shillings and sixpence – not a very good haul from a royal party.

Haymarket, SW1
It is very difficult today to imagine this street being the centre of the market selling hay. The market was established early in the reign of Elizabeth I and was finally removed to Cumberland Market in 1830. A reminder of the elegance of the shops of the eighteenth century can still be seen at number 34, which was originally a snuff shop of the period.

Heath Street, NW3
Hampstead Heath, one of the few remaining wild open spaces in the London area, covering over eight hundred acres, is at one end of the street.

Hemus Place, SW3
Formerly shown as Bedford Place and named from the theatre there, it takes its present name from its builder William Hemus Rayner.

Heneage Lane, EC3
This lane was named after the family which acquired the land here after the dissolution of the nearby monastery of Holy Trinity, Aldgate. In the eighteenth century a synagogue for Spanish and Portuguese Jews was built here to the designs of Mr Avis, a Quaker, who refused to accept any fees. Queen Anne gave a beam for the roof from the royal forests.

Henrietta Place, W1
In 1711, a year after he had purchased the local estate, John Holles, Duke of Newcastle, died as a result of a hunting accident. His daughter, Lady Henrietta Cavendish, inherited the property.

Henrietta Street, WC2
Charles I's queen, Henrietta Maria of France, is remembered here.

Hercules Road, SE1
Where today Christ Church stands, at one end of the road, stood an inn called the Hercules.

Herne Hill, SE24
Lost rivers abound under the streets of London, amongst them the

The Prudential building in Holborn

river Effra. Here was an island or eyot in the river, inhabited by herons.

Highgate
Tollgates were abolished in 1864 but the first one was erected here in the fourteenth century by a local hermit, who was ordered to do so by Edward III in order to pay for the building of the road from this village on the northern heights of London to the City via Holloway.

Hill Street, W1
Several of the streets in this locality led down to the riverbank, where Berkeley Square is today, and so naturally were uneven and hilly. The heads of Sir Thomas Wyatt and three of his companions were exhibited near here in 1554 after their insurrection against Queen Mary failed.

Hogarth Lane, W4
William Hogarth, the painter and engraver, lived in Chiswick and is buried in a tomb in the parish churchyard.

Holborn, EC1
Under the Local Government Act of 1963 the boroughs of Hampstead, Holborn and St Pancras were united into one borough with the new name of Camden. The original area of Holborn takes its name

from the bourne (river) in the hole (hollow), which later in its journey to the Thames becomes the river Fleet.

Holborn Bars, EC1
With the spread of the City in the twelfth century new boundaries were set up and were marked by 'bars'. They became checkpoints for people and vehicles entering or leaving the City.

Holborn Viaduct, EC1
One of the most important street improvements of the Victorian era in the City crosses the steep descent of the banks of the river Fleet. Before construction of the viaduct, between 1863 and 1869, the roadway led through the river. It was the route along which many people, tied to hurdles, were dragged on their way to execution at Tyburn Tree.

Holles Street, W1
In 1710 John Austen sold his Tyburn estate to the Duke of Newcastle, John Holles.

Holloway Road, N7 and N19
Thomas Fuller (1608-61), in his book *Worthies of England*, compliments the hermit of Highgate for excavating Highgate pond and using the gravel to make a causeway in the 'hollow-way' to take travellers safely to the City of London.

Holly Walk, Holly Mount, NW3
Evidence of the long association with the holly bush can still be seen in the vicinity today.

Honey Lane, EC2
Look up at the archway opposite the church of St Mary le Bow in Cheapside and you will see, in the keystone, a bee, the symbol for honey; here was Honey Lane in medieval times.

Hop Gardens, WC2
In his book on Charing Cross, MacMichael says that the name is derived from Sir Hugh Platt's experimental gardens here in the seventeenth century.

Horseferry Road, SW1
Until the building of the first Lambeth Bridge in 1862 a ferry linked the Westminster and Surrey sides of the Thames, carrying horses, coaches and carts across the river. James II and his wife Mary of Modena used the ferry when escaping to France in 1688.

Horse Guards Avenue, SW1
The Horse Guards buildings in Whitehall Palace were originally built in front of the royal palace here as a guard house. In 1753 they were rebuilt by James Gibbs, the noted architect. They house the Household Cavalry when that regiment is on duty.

Hosier Lane, EC1
Appropriately off Smithfield, where one of the great annual events was the cloth fair, hosiers (stocking makers) lived and worked in houses in this lane in the fourteenth century.

Houghton Street, WC2
A house was built here in the seventeenth century by the Holles family, who were also the Barons Houghton.

Houndsditch, EC3
Surrounding the walled area of the City of London was a ditch, or fosse, that formed part of the defences. The hollow was sometimes full of water, but at other times dry, and was also used to dump unwanted articles and other rubbish, including dead dogs.

Howard Road, N16
John Howard, prison reformer and friend of prisoners, came to Stoke Newington in ill health and was nursed with care by his landlady who, in spite of being twenty-seven years his senior, married him.

Hyde Park Crescent, W2
Formerly called Southwick Crescent after Southwick Place, Hampshire, the country seat of the Thistlewayte family, who were lessees of the Paddington manor, today it takes its name from the nearby royal park.

Ilchester Place, W14
The Earls of Ilchester were landowners here in the past.

India Street, EC3
When the East India Company was set up in the late sixteenth century it built East India House in Leadenhall Street and from here ran its business. In 1858, following the reduction of trade with the East Indies, the offices were closed and the company passed to the Crown. In the redevelopment of the area around Fenchurch in the nineteenth century several streets round about were named after the company.

Inner Temple Lane, EC4
Leading under Prince Henry's Room in Fleet Street, the lane takes

the walker into the Inner Temple, past Temple church, and on to the famous gardens of the Temple, where, Shakespeare would have us believe, the Wars of the Roses began. The two opposing families plucked roses, white for York and red for Lancaster, and threw them down as gauntlets in the manner of the challenge at the time.

Ireland Yard, EC4

Land here was once owned by William Ireland. In the archives of the City is a deed of conveyance transferring ownership of a house here to an actor born at Stratford-upon-Avon, one William Shakespeare. The purchase price was £140.

Ironmonger Lane, EC2

Documents of the time of Edward I (1239-1307) show this lane as Ismonger, from the Old English *iren* or *isern* for iron. The original hall of the Ironmongers Company was established here in the fifteenth century but was later bought by the Mercers for an extension of their hall.

Irving Street, WC2

Renamed in the 1930s after the famous ‘actor Sir Henry Irving, whose statue stands behind the National Portrait Gallery, the street was originally called Green Street. Here in the nineteenth century was the curiosity shop that was immortalised by Charles Dickens in one of his novels.

Islington

Whether the name is of Celtic or Belgic origin is uncertain, but the Domesday Book of 1086 refers to it as *Isen*, translated as a spring containing iron, for one such is said to have existed in the neighbourhood at that time. But in the Anglo-Saxon Charters it is written *Gislandune*, meaning the hill or down of Gisla. Its present form dates from the sixteenth century.

Ivy Bridge Lane, WC2

The ivy-clad bridge here was over one of the many small rivers that ran down into the Thames between Westminster and the City.

Jermyn Street, SW1

Once as important a shopping centre as Piccadilly is today, the street laid out by and named after Henry Jermyn, Earl of St Albans, is a back street that still offers goods for the discerning shopper. Here lodged Colonel John Churchill in the seventeenth century, before he won famous victories and became the Duke of Marlborough.

Jerusalem Passage, EC1
This is named from the tavern which stood nearby, itself called after the priory of the Order of St John of Jerusalem.

Jewry Street, EC3
On their return from exile on the continent, Jews resettled here and built for themselves many fine houses. It was one of the few streets of the City to be almost untouched by the Great Fire of 1666, but it did not escape later catastrophes.

John Adam Street, WC2
This is named after one of the Adam brothers who built the Adelphi on the banks of the river Thames in the eighteenth century.

John Carpenter Street, EC4
John Carpenter was town clerk in the fifteenth century, at the time of Sir Richard (Dick) Whittington's mayoralty, and he founded the nearby City of London School for boys.

John Islip Street, SW1
John Islip was the last Abbot of Westminster before the Reformation and was present at the consecration of the new Lady Chapel of the abbey, known today as Henry VII's Chapel, after its founder. Islip's tomb in the abbey carries a rebus of his name in the form of a man falling from a tree and calling out 'I slip'.

Johnson's Court, EC4
Although Dr Samuel Johnson lived here when he was writing *Journey to the Western Islands of Scotland*, the court was named after another person of the same name – Johnson, the Elizabethan antiquarian.

Judges Walk, NW3
While the Great Plague of 1665 was raging in the City and in Westminster, the judges are said to have sat here and slept in tents on the heath.

Junction Mews, Junction Place, W2
Built on land acquired by the Grand Junction Canal Company, the mews still retains a building from 1820, the Boatmen's Institute.

Justice Walk, SW3
Halfway along the Walk is a building, now used as offices and a wine cellar, shown on many maps as the Court House. Here local justice was done, and tradition has it that during the Great Plague of 1665 justice was administered from a tent here.

67

John Keats wrote 'Ode to a Nightingale' at Keats Grove

Kean Street, WC2

After a single performance as Shylock in 1814, the actor Edmund Kean (*c*.1789-1833) was able to move from his humble dwelling here, near Drury Lane Theatre, to better lodgings in Clarges Street.

Keats Grove, NW3

John Keats, poet and man of letters, lived at Wentworth Place from 1818 to 1820. The house is now his museum.

Kemble Street, WC2

Many eighteenth-century actors found fame and fortune on the stage of the Drury Lane Theatre, among them Charles Kemble and his sister, Sarah Siddons.

Kennington Park Road, SE11

When Westminster Bridge was first opened in 1760, what had been a bridlepath was turned into a new road linking the bridge with Brixton, Croydon and Brighton. Kennington Park is all that remains of the grounds of the fourteenth-century palace of the Black Prince.

Kensington

The Kensige family were Saxon inhabitants who have left their name firmly implanted on the map of London. The village of Kemsing in Kent derives its name from the same family.

Kensington Palace Gardens, W8
John Evelyn records in his diary in 1690 that he went to the house that King William III had bought from the Earl of Nottingham and converted into Kensington Palace.

Kensington Square, W8
First built in 1688, it was the principal square in what was then an outer London suburb and is named after the locality.

Kew
The exact origin of the place-name Kew is obscure although there have been a number of attempts to define it. Apart from its modern spelling, eight different forms can be traced in various documents. In the Court Roll of Richmond, at the time of Henry VII it is written *Kayhough*, and *Keyhoe* during the reign of Henry VIII. In later documents it is variously given as *Kayhowe*, *Kyahoe*, *Keyhowe*, *Keye*, *Kaiho* and *Kewe*. *Key* or 'quay' may well give a vital clue to its origin, and the fact that *hoo*, *hough* and *ho* could well be linked with *hoe*, meaning a level place by the waterside, should also be taken into account: 'a quay, or landing place, by a level stretch or riverbank'.

Kilburn Park Road, NW6
The earliest mention of the name appears in the reign of Henry I (1068-1135), when a hermit settled near a small stream called, in various records, 'Cuneburne', 'Keelebourne', 'Coldburne' and 'Kilbourne'. This is the same stream that later becomes the Westbourne.

King Edward Street, EC1
Previously known as Blowbladder Street after the butchers' practice of making their meat look fatter by means of inflating a bladder inside the carcase, it is shown later as Stinking Lane, because of the proximity of the slaughterhouse. It was renamed when Edward VII officially opened the new buildings for the General Post Office.

King Henry's Walk, N16
Henry VII had a hunting lodge nearby in the sixteenth century when the area was surrounded by forests.

King's Bench Walk, EC4
In the eighteenth century the King's Bench Office was situated here. Many of the houses here date from the seventeenth and

King's Bench Walk

eighteenth centuries, although a few have had to be rebuilt because of bombing in the Second World War.

King's Cross, N1
The area took its name from the monument at the crossroads on which stood a statue of George IV.

King's Road, SW3
Originally a footway through the fields that developed into a roadway for the private use of Charles II, it was taken over by the local vestry in 1831 and is now Chelsea's high street.

King Street, SW1
Fields in the area were laid out as streets, lanes and squares in 1673. This street commemorates Charles II and his brother, the Duke of York, afterwards James II.

King Street, WC2
Laid out in 1637 as part of the general development of the area by Inigo Jones, the street was named as a compliment to Charles I, the reigning monarch. The statue of Charles I by Le

Sueur was first erected here, but at the end of the Civil War it was sold to a Holborn blacksmith for making into souvenirs for loyal royalists. However, at the restoration of the monarchy in 1660 it was brought to light again, having been buried in the smith's garden.

Kingsway, WC2
Opened by Edward VII, the street was so named after several suggestions had been submitted. Originally it formed part of Theobalds Road, which now starts at the end of Kingsway.

King William Street, EC4
Not one of the most architecturally distinguished streets of London (practically all of it has been rebuilt since 1914), it was one of the new roadways brought about by the building of the nine-teenth-century London Bridge by Rennie and was opened by William IV, whose statue once stood at the junction of the street with Gracechurch Street.

Kirby Street, EC1
In the thirteenth century Bishop Kirby of Ely built a palace just outside the City Wall. It was the London home of the Bishops of Ely until the sixteenth century when the incumbent bishop was obliged by Queen Elizabeth I to surrender it to her favourite, Sir Christopher Hatton.

Knightrider Street, EC4
According to Stow, knights used the street when riding 'well armed and mounted' from the Tower of London to the King's Wardrobe or, perhaps, to Baynards Castle.

Knightsbridge, SW1 and SW7
Eleventh-century evidence indicates a bridge here over the river Westbourne known as *Cnichtebrugge*, which has been translated as 'the bridge of the serving boy'. Traditionally the bridge belongs to those knights who were going off to war but first went to Fulham to receive a blessing from the Bishop of London in the chapel of his palace there.

Lambeth
Shown on maps and in ancient charters as 'Lamb's Hythe' or 'lambhythe', a hithe being a dock or harbour, Lambeth was therefore a place where lambs were shipped in or out.

Harrods department store in Knightsbridge

Lamb's Conduit Street, WC1

Conduits were once commonplace in London and the one here was built in 1577 by William Lambe, described as a gentleman of the King's Chapel and a clothworker of London. His contribution to the welfare of his fellow citizens is duly recorded in the street's name.

Lammas Road, E9

The name recalls the ancient practice of enclosing the local agricultural land between Lady Day (25th March) and Lammas Day (1st August), during which time crops could be grown. On the latter day all the fences were taken down and the open pasturage was restored. Lammas Fields now form part of the open space of the borough.

Lancaster Place, WC2

This is within the liberty (area free from law and taxes) of the Duke of Lancaster and where the office of that Duchy is still situated.

Lansdowne Passage, W1

In the eighteenth century Robert Adam designed, for the Marquis of Bute, Lansdowne House, most of which was demolished in

1921. Behind the site runs a passage once notorious as an escape route for footpads and highwaymen. To put a stop to this abuse, bar gates were erected at each end and they are still there today.

Larkhall Rise, Larkhall Lane, SW4
Wyld's map of the area in 1844 shows 'Lark Hall Tea Gardens' and *The Ambulator* of 1860 makes reference to the erection of houses nearby. Number 5 in the Rise was the birthplace in 1861 of Cardinal Bourne, the Roman Catholic Archbishop of Westminster. On his death in 1935 he was buried in his cathedral at Westminster.

Laurence Pountney Hill, EC4
Here was built in the eleventh century a church that was dedicated to St Laurence. It was rebuilt with a college in the fourteenth century by Sir John Pountney.

Lawrence Street, SW3
Here in the eighteenth century was the Chelsea Pottery. The street name reminds us of a lord of the manor whose home was demolished in the early part of the same century.

Laycock Street, N1
Before his death in 1834 Charles Laycock was well-known for his large dairy farm here.

Leadenhall Street, Leadenhall Market, EC3
Where the present market (rebuilt in the nineteenth century) now stands, there was once a manor house built by Sir Hugh Nevill in 1309. Its main roof was covered with lead. Sir Richard Whittington, Lord Mayor of London on four separate occasions in the fifteenth century, bought the house and lived in it for a time.

Leather Lane, EC1
In 1241 the lane was known as *le Vrunlane*, from the Flemish, meaning 'Stoke Lane', for it led to the fields of the Stoke of Portpoole. By Stow's time, the sixteenth century, the name is shown as Lither Lane, which is but a short step to Leather Lane.

Leicester Square, WC2
Between 1635 and 1671 a mansion was built by the Earl of Leicester in the Leicester Fields, on land owned by the Sidney family. This became Leicester Square at the beginning of the eighteenth century.

*Leicester
Square*

The Lammas dues (parish rates) for the house and gardens are shown in records as being £3. During the century of the square's formation William Hogarth came to live in a house, later occupied by the Archbishop Tenison Grammar School for boys, in the south-east corner of the square. Sir Joshua Reynolds, founder and first President of the Royal Academy, lived and died at number 47.

Lime Street, EC3
According to Stow the name originates from the makers of lime in the vicinity, but it could also come from the Saxon word for 'dirty' – although there were few streets that could be called clean in medieval London. The street was a fashionable place to live in the eighteenth century.

Limeburner Lane, EC4
The lane recalls the occupancy of the medieval limeburners, who settled outside the city wall and on the bank of the river Fleet. Lime (quicklime) was obtained by heating limestone in a kiln and when water was applied the stone broke up to form a white powder. The stench drove the workers out of the City to the riverside. The finished product was then sold in Lime Street.

Lincoln's Inn Fields, WC2
On a piece of land owned by the Earls of Lincoln 'without the wall of the city by Oldbourne', the Blackfriars (Dominicans) were first established in London. Later some of the area was given over to the 'men of learning and law' and one of the great Inns of Court was founded. Inigo Jones, the noted Palladian architect, laid out the fields in 1618 and built a series of houses round about. One of the original houses, numbers 59 and 60, remains, but the others have all been replaced over the years. The fields were once used as a place of execution and Lord William Russell was beheaded

here in 1683 for his part in the Rye House Plot. They also became famous as a duelling ground. Today the twelve acres are owned and maintained by the borough of Camden for the enjoyment of all.

Lisson Grove, NW1
Lilleston was once the tonship (township) of the Lille family and the modern variant of the name is Lisson.

Little Britain, EC1
The Dukes of Brittany established themselves here early in the fourteenth century. Later the street became the abode of book-sellers and publishers, and many books of the seventeenth and eighteenth centuries bear the imprint 'sold in Little Britain at the sign of...'. From a shop here John Milton's *Paradise Lost* was first published, and the first copy of *The Spectator* was published here in 1711.

Little Venice, W9
After the death of his wife, Elizabeth Barrett, in 1862, Robert Browning (1812-89) settled on the banks of the Grand Junction Canal in Paddington. He said that the view reminded him of Venice, where they had spent many pleasurable days together.

A canal boat festival at Little Venice

Loddiges Road, E9

Rhubarb was first grown and sold here in the eighteenth century, by a market gardener named Conrad Loddiges.

Lollard Street, SE11

Followers of John Wycliffe, who translated the Bible into English in 1382 and 1388, were imprisoned in a tower at Lambeth Palace. They were known as Lollards and the tower is also called the Lollards' Tower after them.

Lombard Street, EC3

Following the expulsion of Jews from England in the thirteenth century their place as moneylenders and bankers was taken by men from Lombardy, who were then recognised as the financial experts of the continent. Their influence continued until the sixteenth century, by which time English merchants had gained sufficient knowledge of banking to take over from the Lombards.

London Fields, E8

At the dissolution of the priory of Clerkenwell in 1541 some sixty acres of its property were confiscated by Henry VIII. They have been called the Shoulder of Mutton Fields, from a local tavern, but today they are known as the fields near London.

London Wall, EC2

Towards the end of the second century AD the Romans built a wall round London from the east side (by where the Tower of London now stands) to the site of Blackfriars. It enclosed 330 acres, making *Londinium* the fifth largest city in the Roman Empire.

Long Acre, WC2

Formerly called the Elms, this was a public footpath opened in 1612 and stretching for a long acre. A resident here between 1637 and 1643 was a certain Captain Oliver Cromwell. Later in the same century the coachmakers settled here. Samuel Pepys had his own coach made here and records his visits in his diary.

Long Lane, EC1

The lane is appropriately named, for by City standards it is a lengthy street. John Stow refers to it as being 'truly long'.

Lord North Street, SW1

This was laid out *c*.1722 and shown at that time as North Street, being on the north side of the square from which it leads.

Ludgate Hill, by Gustave Doré

Lothbury, EC2

Here were to be found the Worshipful Company of Founderers, in Founderers Court, and the pewterers and metalworkers, all of whom made a loathsome noise and smell. The street, which once crossed the Walbrook, was once also lived in by the 'Lod', 'Loda' or 'Loppa' people.

Lovat Lane, EC3

For his part in the abortive 1745 uprising in Scotland Lord Lovat was beheaded on Tower Hill – the last to suffer that fate publicly.

Lower Marsh and Upper Marsh, SE1

This area was once liable to be flooded by the river and, although this was beneficial to the kitchen gardens, it was one of the last areas to be built on in the growth of London's south bank district.

Lower Thames Street, EC3

Combined with Upper Thames Street, this formerly riverside roadway is the longest in the City, stretching from the Tower of London to Blackfriars.

Ludgate Hill, Ludgate Circus, EC4

Leading to an ancient gateway into the City, it takes its name from the word *ludda* meaning 'postern' or 'back gate'. Some writers say that King Lud, the ancient founder of the City – 'Ludds Town' – gave his name to the gate and the hill. However, evidence of this king is sadly lacking, although a statue of him and two of his sons, which once stood on Ludgate itself, can still be seen, beside one of Elizabeth I, by the side of the church of St Dunstan in the West, Fleet Street.

Lupus Street, SW1

An ancestor of the Dukes of Westminster was Hugh Lupus, Earl of Chester.

Lyons Place, NW8

This preserves the name of the founder of Harrow School whose estates here helped finance the school in its early days.

Macaulay Road, SW4

In Church Buildings nearby there was once a school for black boys brought to England by Zachary Macaulay. But the English weather did not agree with them and they were sent back home. Later the school was attended by Macaulay's son, Thomas Babington Macaulay, the famous historian.

Macklin Street, WC2

A great actor, Charles Macklin 'balmed his stomach with a pint of stout sweetened to a syrup' and lived in Bow Street.

Admiralty Arch at the north end of the Mall

Maddox Street, W1

Sir Benjamin Maddox, who died in 1670, was the original land-owner, but the street was laid out in the eighteenth century for the Earl of Burlington.

Maida Vale, W9

Commanded by General Sir John Stuart, the British Army defeated Napoleon's army in battle at Maida in Italy in 1806. The hero of the battle was the general, even though he commanded the fighting from the rear.

Maiden Lane, WC2

The name is most probably derived from the 'middens' (refuse heaps) that were common sights throughout London's history.

The Mall, SW1

Laid out originally in the late seventeenth century, after the return to England of Charles II, the avenue with four lines of trees was once attributed to the design of Andre Le Notre. Its name originates, like Pall Mall, from the French lawn game *pale-maille* that was played nearby.

Manchester Square, Manchester Street, W1

George Montagu, fourth Duke of Manchester, built himself a mansion here in the eighteenth century. Today his house, Hertford House, contains the Wallace Collection of fine and decorative art.

Manette Street, W1
Doctor Manette, a character in Charles Dickens's book *A Tale of Two Cities*, lived nearby in number 1, Greek Street.

Mansion House Place, Mansion House Street, EC4
Until the building in 1739 of an official residence for the Lord Mayor, he usually used his own company's hall for entertaining. Since that time Mansion House has served as the Lord Mayor's home in the City.

Marcilly Road, SW18
This was once known as St Anne's Road after the dedication of the local parish church. It was changed to commemorate the mistress, and second wife, of the second Viscount Bolingbroke – Marie Claire des Champs de Marcilly.

Mare Street, E8
A large pond fed by the Hackney Brook caused constant trouble to coaches and their passengers in the eighteenth century. Because of its low-lying nature the area around Mare Street was a marsh and the street is called Mere (marsh) Street on early maps.

Margaret Street, W1
Lady Margaret Cavendish, later the wife of Lord Harley, inherited the estate from her father.

Mark Lane, EC3
Leading out of Great Tower Street, an extension of Eastcheap (a medieval market), it is not hard to imagine this lane as a mart or market, although some authorities would have us believe that a lady whose name was Martha lived here.

Marshalsea Road, SE1
Nineteenth-century London had a great many prisons, judging by the vivid account of such places in the novels of the time. One of the best-known was Marshalsea Prison, here in the Borough, where Charles Dickens's father was sent for bankruptcy.

Marsham Street, SW1
Charles Marsham, Earl of Romney, began the building of the street in 1688.

Marylebone Lane, W1
Running through an old village, St Mary's by the Bourne (river), it
was once known as Lusty Lane.

Mason's Avenue, EC2
The Masons' Hall was once situated on one side of this avenue, which
connects Coleman Street and Basinghall Street. James I came here on a
number of occasions to visit Dr William Butler – the tavern here still bears
his name – who, instead of prescribing pharmaceutical compounds, gave
his patients his special brew of beer to drink.

Matthew Parker Street, SW1
An eminent Archbishop of Canterbury in the sixteenth century, Matthew
Parker was the seventy-first occupant of St Augustine's chair.

Melbury Road, W14
The Dukes of Ilchester, ground landlords of Kensington, held
property in the Dorset village of Melbury.

Middle Temple Lane, EC4
Leading down to the Embankment from Fleet Street, the lane
contains some very interesting seventeenth-century buildings, particularly at the upper end. Just under the arch of the gatehouse,
built in 1684 to the designs of an amateur architect of the Middle
Temple, Roger North, can be found the old post office, round
whose pillars Dr Johnson used to swing. Halfway down the lane is
Middle Temple Hall, dating from 1574 and a fine example of
Tudor architecture. Here Elizabeth I witnessed the first performance
of Shakespeare's *Twelfth Night* early in the seventeenth century.
Further down still is the fine wrought ironwork of the gateway into
the Temple. Middle Temple itself is between the Inner and Outer
Temples. Once the home of the Knights Templars, today it is the
working and living quarters of the 'men of law and their students'.

Mildmay Road, Mildmay Park, N1
On the south side of Newington Green stood Mildmay House, the
residence of Sir Henry Mildmay, one of the regicides who con-
demned Charles I. The site is now occupied by a hospital.

Milk Street, EC2
Sir (Saint) Thomas More was born in 1478 in a house in this street,
which housed the sellers of milk in medieval times.

Millbank, SW1
Once a slum beyond the abbey and palace at Westminster, this stretch

of the riverside was redeveloped during the construction of the embankment in 1871. Here stood in medieval times the water and wind mills of the abbey. Today Imperial Chemicals House, designed by Sir Frank Baines and built between 1929 and 1931, dominates the street.

Mill Lane, NW6
In 1861 the mill which stood at the junction with the Edgware Road was destroyed by a fire caused by the high velocity of the sails in a gale.

Mill Street, W1
Here is a reminder of more rural times when a mill stood on the corner of what is today Hanover Square.

Milner Square, N1
A friend of Charles Dickens and Disraeli and an active politician, Thomas Milner (1806-84) owned many acres in Islington.

Milton Street, EC2
One of the City's greatest sons, John Milton (1608-74), was born in Bread Street and lived for the last twelve years of his life in nearby Bunhill Fields and Bunhill Row. He was buried in St Giles's church, Cripplegate.

Mincing Lane, EC3
Stow's *Survay* shows this lane as 'Michums' and mentions tenements (houses) of the nuns of St Helen's church and convent in Bishopsgate.

Minories, EC3
The minoresses were the nuns of the Order of St Clare who founded a convent here in 1293. It stood outside the City wall in the liberty of the

Millbank

Tower of London. The Order was suppressed at the time of the dissolution of the monasteries in the sixteenth century by Henry VIII. Later some of the area was used as a detention camp for prisoners taken after the battle of Culloden Field in 1745, and many soldiers died and were buried here.

Mint Street, SE1
In the time of Henry VIII a mint was set up here.

Mitre Court, EC4
One of Dr Samuel Johnson's favourite taverns, the Mitre was demolished in the nineteenth century, and the site is now marked with a City Corporation blue plaque.

Mitre Street, Mitre Square, EC3
Standing on the site of the former Holy Trinity Priory, Aldgate, both the street and the square take their name from the Mitre Tavern that succeeded the monastery, whose abbot wore a mitre – normally the headpiece of a bishop – as a sign of his office.

Monmouth Road, W2
Royal associations with Paddington include the residence there from 1675 to 1678 of the Duke of Monmouth, son of Charles II.

Montague Close, SE1
Lying between Southwark Cathedral and London Bridge, the close is built on the site of the domestic quarters of the former Augustinian priory which stood here from the twelfth to the sixteenth centuries. At the dissolution the land was bought by Viscount Montague, who, 'being of the Old Faith', continued to worship here after the Reformation.

Monument Street, EC3
The realignment of the streets around London Bridge brought into being this street whose dominant landmark is the Monument. This was built to the design of Sir Christopher Wren between 1671 and 1677 and commemorates the Great Fire of London of 1666. It stands, it is said, 202 feet from where the fire started and reaches the same distance into the sky.

Moorfields, EC2
Writing in the twelfth century, Fitzstephen, secretary to Archbishop Thomas Becket, tells of the moor or marsh outside the City wall. It was, he says, used for gatherings, lawful and otherwise, in the

summer months, while in the winter it became an open-air ice-rink. The Walbrook river, which started in these fields, overflowed and for several weeks froze solid, enabling the apprentices, ever resourceful, to tie the bones of animals to their shoes and skate across the ice.

Moorgate, EC2
In Roman days there was a postern (back) gate, where later, in 1415, Thomas Falconer, Lord Mayor of London 1414-15, had a gatehouse built. The street taking its name from this old City gate stretches from the northern boundary of the City at Finsbury Pavement to Lothbury in the south.

Moravian Close, SW3
In the eighteenth century Count Zinzendorf of Saxony installed the Brotherhood of Moravians in Chelsea. The close leads to their burial ground.

Motcomb Street, SW1
Dowager Marchionesses of Westminster have a Dorset estate which includes the village of Motcombe.

Mount Street, W1
Part of the outer defences of London in the seventeenth century, erected by order of Oliver Cromwell, was a series of mounds where travellers could be halted, checked and searched. This mount guarded the approaches from the west of the City.

Muscovy Street, EC3
Ambassadors from Muscovy (Russia) had living quarters here in the sixteenth century and in the mid seventeenth century Czar Peter the Great frequented the local tavern so often that it was renamed the Czar of Muscovy's Head.

Museum Street, WC1
The street connects Bloomsbury Way with Great Russell Street, the home of the British Museum.

Myddleton Street, EC1
Sir Hugh Myddleton was the 'great water benefactor', engineering the conveyance of drinking water from Amwell in Hertfordshire to the New River Head reservoirs close to Sadlers Wells Theatre in Rosebery Avenue.

Nelsons Row, SW4
Tradition has it that Lord Nelson stayed at an inn in Clapham.

New Bridge Street, EC4
This leads from Blackfriars Bridge, the second bridge owned by the City (London Bridge was the first). The street was first constructed in 1760 over the line of the river Fleet, which still flows under it today.

New End, NW3
Villages around London grew vastly in the eighteenth century and newly built-up areas were added to the older parts. There are still a number of houses in the vicinity dating from this growth.

Newgate Street, EC1
Shown on some early maps as Chamberlain Gate, the street takes its name from the gate in the City wall made by the Romans in the second century. The gate housed the notorious Newgate prison, established in the reign of King John. It was rebuilt with money left by Dick Whittington in the fifteenth century. At the time of the 'No Popery' riots in the eighteenth century extensive damage was done to the prison and it is said that during the riots the keys of the prison were thrown into a pool in St James's Square.

Newington Green, N16 and N1
Created in the middle ages out of part of the former Middlesex Forest, the green remained relatively clear until the seventeenth century when hunting lodges were built nearby. After the passing of the Act of Uniformity in 1662, the area became a centre of nonconformity.

New Oxford Street, WC1
A busy commercial thoroughfare opened after slum clearance in 1847, it formed a useful bypass to the nearby village of St Giles's.

Newport Street, Great and Little, WC2
Lord Newport had a mansion here at the time of Charles II.

'New Road', W2
In 1756 it was decided to build what was to become London's first bypass, the New Road. The intention of the builders was to divert from Bayswater Road and Oxford Road (Street) the cattle which were interfering with the progress of 'my lady's coach' on its journey to and from London. The road, which is now Sussex Gardens, Marylebone (Old) Road, Euston Road and City Road, led the cattle away from the coaches and directly to the slaughter-houses and the market of Smithfield. But, alas, the ladies also

The view in 1869 of the building of the Thames embankment

from Somerset House to the Temple steamboat quay

discovered that it was quicker to use the new road, and soon that too became crowded.

New Square, Lincoln's Inn, WC2
Lying on the south side of the Inn of Court, New Square was built in the seventeenth century. It forms a pleasant oasis for lawyers and law students.

Nicholas Lane, Nicholas Passage, EC4
In 1666 the Great Fire destroyed many churches, including that of St Nicholas Acons. The church, which had been founded in the twelfth century, was not rebuilt after the fire.

Noble Street, EC2
In the Calendar of Coroners of London in 1322 appears the name of Thomas Le Noble, whose ownership of the property here gave rise to the street name. Robert Tichborne, a signatory to Charles I's death warrant, lived here; he was Lord Mayor of London in 1657.

Northampton Road, EC1
One of a number of streets and roads named after the ground landlord, the Marquess of Northampton, is shown on seventeenth-century maps as a rural, tree-lined avenue.

Northumberland Avenue, WC2; Northumberland Alley, EC3
Both streets, the former at Charing Cross and the latter in the City, derive their names from the town residences of the Earls of Northumberland.

Notting Hill, W11 and W2
'Here we go gathering nuts in May' is an old nursery rhyme, and it has been suggested that 'nuts' – branches from hazel trees – were collected from the hill on the eve of May Day.

Oakley Street, SW3
Sir Hans Sloane, whose books and *objets d'art* formed the nucleus of the British Museum's collections, had no sons to succeed him. He divided his estate between his two daughters, Sarah and Elizabeth, the latter marrying Lord Cadogan of Oakley. Part of the street runs through the grounds occupied by Whitehall Palace, built on the river's edge by Henry VIII.

Observatory Gardens, W8
Sir Henry South, the noted astronomer, had a fully equipped observatory here from 1836 until his death in 1867.

Old Bailey, EC4

Although the use of the name here dates from the middle of the thirteenth century, 'bailey' is an ancient word for an open space in front of a city wall or an enclosed area of a castle or other fortification.

Old Compton Street, W1

Named after Bishop Compton, the street becomes an open-air market or labour exchange for waiters every Monday morning.

Old Jewry, EC2

This was so called because the Jews lived in this quarter of the City from the eleventh century, when they were established in London by William the Conqueror, until their expulsion in the late thirteenth century by Edward I. It was also the scene of Jewish massacres in 1261 and 1264. On their return in the seventeenth century, under the protection of William III, a synagogue was built here, although they also settled elsewhere in the City.

Old Mitre Court, EC4

A City Corporation blue plaque marks the site of the old Mitre Tavern in Fleet Street, beside which is the court where once stood the famous Mitre Coffee House.

Old Palace Yard, SW1

In 1834 fire destroyed the old Westminster Palace, which was afterwards rebuilt to the designs of Sir Charles Barry. The yard marks the site of one of the inner courts. Another reminder of the former royal palace stands nearby – the Jewel Tower. Here, too, the executions of Sir Walter Raleigh and Guy Fawkes took place in the seventeenth century.

Old Pye Street, SW1

During the time of the Commonwealth the estates of Westminster Abbey were vested in a committee under the chairmanship of Sir Robert Pye. A prominent member of the local vestry, he lived at Stourton House nearby.

Old Town, SW4

Around the former parish church of Clapham, now St Paul's Rectory Grove, the old village grew, until in the eighteenth century it outgrew its original site and the centre moved to around the new church on the common.

Onslow Square, Onslow Gardens, SW7
The ground landlord was the Earl of Onslow.

Orange Street, WC2
Built in the late seventeenth century to honour the Dutch house of Orange, when James II's daughter Mary and her husband William of Orange, both Protestants, became joint monarchs after her Catholic father had been driven from the throne.

Orchard Street, W1
The Portman family, who developed this area in the eighteenth century, took the title of this street from their village in Somerset, Orchard Portman.

Oxenden Street, SW1
Sir Henry Oxenden married the daughter of Robert Baker, a tailor who built Piccadilly Hall, and developed the estate around the house.

Oxford Court, off Walbrook and Salters Court, EC4
The name commemorates the site of the former town house of the Earls of Oxford.

Oxford Square, W2
A local resident, the Countess of Richmond, was a generous benefactor of the University of Oxford.

Oxford Street, W1
Various names are shown on maps – Tyburn Road, Road to Oxford, Road to Worcester, Oxford Road, Tiburn Road – until 1720 when 'Oxford Street' appeared for the first time. Today it is one of London's most popular shopping streets.

Paddington
Here during Saxon times the Paeda family settled and set up a farm or homestead (ton) nearby. The addition of the family name to 'ton' produced the present name.

Paddington Green, W2
Villages are often centred around a village green and Paddington is no exception. Here the parish church and one or two other old buildings still stand. Nearby stage-coaches picked up and set down their passengers; here, too, Shillibeer started the first omnibus service in London in 1829. For a fare of one shilling customers could ride in comfort on the horse-drawn coach to the Bank, and even if the journey did sometimes take three hours, there were

Pall Mall about 1740

always the papers to read, for they were part of the service.

Page Street, SW1
Doctor William Page was the headmaster of Westminster School early in the nineteenth century.

Pall Mall, SW1
Returning to London from exile in France, Charles II introduced the French game of *pale-maille* to the English royal court. The game was similar to crocquet except that instead of a mallet a pole with a hoop at one end is used to propel the ball. Pepys, in his diary entry for 26th July 1660, refers to it as Pall Mall and tells how he and some friends spent the evening at Wood's, a tavern nearby. The only seventeenth-century house to survive is Schomberg House, built for the Duke of Schomberg, who was killed at the Battle of the Boyne in 1690.

Palmer Street, SW1
Until they were demolished in 1881, almshouses founded by the Reverend James Palmer in 1654 stood here. They were amalgamated with the Westminster United Almshouses, Rochester Row, in 1887.

Pancras Lane, EC4
Destroyed in the Great Fire and not rebuilt, the parish church of St Pancras stood here in the middle ages.

Panton Street, SW1
Colonel Panton, a great gambler, lived in the neighbourhood. He died in 1681.

Panyer Alley Steps, EC4

Leading to the Paternoster Square development, the Steps commemorate the Panyer Boy, an inn whose seventeenth-century sign shows the baker's errand boy with his pannier or basket. However, the accompanying verse, which tells the reader that 'when he has sought the City round, this is still the highest ground', is wrong – Cornhill is higher than Ludgate by a few inches.

Park Crescent, W1

The crescent forms the end of the route of royal processions from Carlton House to Regent's Park.

Park Lane, W1

Few London streets can have a better view than that from Park Lane across Hyde Park itself. The lane was called Tyburn Lane and led to the dreaded Tyburn Tree, the gallows which stood at the junction of Edgware Road, Bayswater Road and Oxford Street.

Park Place, SW1

Built in 1683, this is a pleasant cul-de-sac leading to the buildings which line the Queen's Walk of Green Park.

Park Street, W1

Shown on the maps of the late eighteenth century as Hyde Park Street, it was one of the later developments in this area.

Parliament Square, SW1

Part of the new approach roads to Westminster Bridge, first built in 1750, the square is dominated by the Houses of Parliament and Westminster Abbey. The square was the site of the first roundabout system for traffic in London.

Parliament Street, SW1

This street connects Whitehall with Parliament Square and leads to the Houses of Parliament. It is often mistakenly considered to form part of Whitehall, but the Cenotaph marks the junction of the two streets. The houses on the south side are all that remains of those built about 1753 when the street was first laid out.

Passing Alley, EC1

This leads from St John's Lane to St John's Street, passing through buildings at either end.

St Paul's Cathedral seen from the Millennium Bridge.

Passmore Street, SW1
Richard Passmore, a carpenter, obtained permission in 1833 to build a street on lease from the Grosvenor estate.

Paternoster Square, EC4
Lying to the north of St Paul's Cathedral, the square crosses the path taken by medieval pilgrims and others when on festive procession round the precincts of the cathedral, reciting the rosary on the way. Here was the station at which they repeated the *Pater Noster* – Our Father.

Paultons Square, SW3
Sarah, daughter of Sir Hans Sloane (1660-1753), married George Stanley of Paultons in Hampshire. Sloane's two daughters were heirs to his vast Chelsea estate.

The Pavement, SW4
Paved footpaths in towns or villages were rare until the late nineteenth century, but during the eighteenth century this street was covered with paving-stones.

Paxton Road, W4
Joseph Paxton designed many great glasshouses, including one in the grounds of Chiswick House and his first at Chatsworth, Derbyshire, but he is best known for the Crystal Palace he built for the Great Exhibition in Hyde Park in 1851.

Peabody Avenue, SW1
George Peabody was an American philanthropist who, in the nineteenth century, built a number of housing estates for the working class of London.

Pepys Street, EC3
We owe much of our knowledge of life in the seventeenth century to the diary of Samuel Pepys, Secretary to the Navy Office. He lived in Seething Lane, opposite the church of St Olave, Hart Street, where he and his wife, Elizabeth, are buried.

Peter's Hill, EC4
A church was first erected here in the twelfth century, but it was not rebuilt after the Great Fire. St Peter's churchyard is commemorated today by an inscription on a modern wall.

Peter's Lane, EC1
It is listed in Stow's *Survay* as St Peter's Lane – the lane of St Peter's church – and a nearby tavern was called the Cross Keys, the sign of St Peter in medieval times. Today the building is an office, but the sign remains. Opposite the lane is the site of Hicks Hall, the former Sessions House, built by Sir Baptist Hicks in the seventeenth century.

'Petticoat Lane' (Middlesex Street), E1
Ladies' petticoats were once sold in the clothiers' market here in a street that used to mark the boundary between the City of London and Middlesex, a former county area. A market still flourishes here, particularly on a Sunday morning.

Petty France, SW1
After the Edict of Nantes in 1685 many French refugees settled here, around an area where in the previous century French wool merchants had set up a colony for trading purposes.

Philpot Lane, EC3
Grocer and Alderman of Langbourne Ward, Sir John Philpot, Lord Mayor of London in 1378 and member of parliament for the City, built himself a mansion here. On his death in 1384 he was buried in the choir of the Grey Friars church in Newgate Street.

Piccadilly, W1
Piccadilly takes its name from a form of collar or ruff called a 'piccadil', made by a tailor in nearby Haymarket in the early seventeenth century. The designer of this garment, a certain Mr Higgins, built himself a house here and called it Piccadilly Hall. The place was described as being 'a fair house for entertainment and gaming, with handsome gravel walks, and an upper and lower bowling green'.

Pickering Place, SW1
Hidden behind the wine merchants Berry Brothers & Rudd is an unspoilt Georgian backwater of London. William Pickering built this quiet oasis for himself from the profits of the coffee business he founded. Lord Palmerston lived here for a time, as did Lord Byron. It was from his house here that Byron went to the House of Lords to make his first and only speech in the House.

Pilgrim Street, EC4
Before the Reformation Old St Paul's Cathedral contained relics of saints, which attracted many pilgrims there.

Playhouse Yard, EC4
This marks the site of the Blackfriars Theatre, which used the refectory of the old monastery. The playhouse was used by theatrical companies, including William Shakespeare's, in winter when theatres such as the Globe and the Rose on Bankside, Southwark, were rendered unusable by the weather.

Plough Court, EC3
In this court, which takes its name from a tavern that stood here, Alexander Pope was born in 1688.

Pond Square, N6
The pond here was dug by the same hermit who built the causeway along the hollow-way (Holloway Road). Here Sir Francis Bacon froze a chicken for the first time and the bird is said still to haunt the square. Unfortunately Sir Francis caught pneumonia and died as a result of the experiment.

Pond Street, NW3
According to Rocque's map, dating from the eighteenth century, the local cattle pound stood here.

Pont Street, SW1
This was named from the bridge (*pont* in French) over the nearby river Westbourne, which no longer flows above ground but beneath the streets.

A busker in Portobello Road

Pope's Head Alley, EC3

According to John Stow's *Survay of the Cities of London and Westminster*, first published in 1598, at the foot of Cornhill stood a royal palace that was later used as a hostel (house) by the Earls of Suffolk. In turn it became a tavern with the sign of the Pope's Head. In spite of the Reformation of the sixteenth century the tavern did not change its name and it survived until the mid eighteenth century.

Poppins Court, EC4

This was formerly shown as 'Poppinjay' from the crest of the Abbots of Cirencester, who had their town house close by in the middle ages.

Portland Place, W1

Designed by the Adam brothers in the eighteenth century and later used by John Nash as part of the processional route to Regent's Park, the street commemorates the Dukes of Portland, whose land it is.

Portman Square, W1

Having inherited part of St Marylebone in the eighteenth century, Henry William Portman, of Orchard Portman in Somerset, developed the estate by speculative building.

Portobello Road, W10 and W11

Farms and fields are far removed from the heavily populated area of Notting Hill today. But in 1739, following the capture of the town of Porto Bello on the Gulf of Mexico by Admiral Vernon, a local farmer called Adams renamed his farm in honour of the victory. These days the street is famous for the Saturday antiques market.

Portpool Lane, EC1
Originally the present Gray's Inn Road was shown by this name, which comes from a pond or pool outside the gate of the City.

Portsmouth Street, WC2
When Inigo Jones laid out Lincoln's Inn Fields in the seventeenth century, he designed a house here for the Earl of Portsmouth. Whether or not the Old Curiosity Shop here is the one referred to by Charles Dickens in his book is not known.

Portugal Street, WC2
This is one of a number of streets named in honour of Charles II's Portuguese queen, Catharine of Braganza.

Post Office Court, EC3
The headquarters of the General Post Office were here from its inception in 1656 until 1829 when it moved to Newgate Street.

Powell's Walk, W4
Once the manor of Chiswick belonged to the Dean and Chapter of St Paul's Cathedral – they still appoint the vicar of St Nicholas's parish church – and the walk was then called St Paul's Walk. 'Powell's' is a corruption of 'Paul's'.

Powis Place, WC1
At the end of the seventeenth century the second Marquis of Powis built himself a mansion where Great Ormond Street runs today. It was burnt down in 1713.

Praed Street, W2
The first chairman of the Grand Junction Canal Company was William Praed, a banker. The canal, opened in 1801, terminated nearby.

Priestley Close, N16
Joseph Priestley, the eminent scientist who discovered oxygen, was minister of South Hackney Unitarian church in 1792.

Primrose Hill, NW3
Rising to a height of 216 feet, the hill commands a magnificent view. Originally shown as Barrow Hill, from the prehistoric burial here, the present name dates from Elizabethan times and is said to derive from the primroses which grew here in profusion.

Prince's Street, EC2
This is a royal companion for King Street and Queen Street. All three streets were laid out after the Great Fire of London in 1666.

Printing House Square, EC4
Between 1788 and 1974 *The Times* newspaper was printed here. The square is built on part of the land occupied by the Dominican priory of Black Friars.

Priory Road, NW6
When the London & North Western Railway was being built relics of a priory, founded in the twelfth century by Godwyn, were discovered here.

Prout Road, E5
The author of the most comprehensive set of books on musical theory, Dr Ebenezer Prout, lived in Navarina Road. His revised edition of Handel's *Messiah* is still in constant use today.

Provost Road, NW3
On land once owned by Eton College, whose headmaster is the Provost, it is appropriately named.

Pudding Lane, EC3
Butchers from Eastcheap sent pudding, or offal, from their shops down this lane on its way to the dung boats on the Thames. Earlier names of the lane were Rethergate, Rotherlane and Red Rose, from a tavern nearby. The lane's greatest claim to fame is that the Great Fire of London of 1666 started here in the shop of the king's baker.

Puddle Dock, EC4
Beside the Mermaid theatre was once to be found Puddle Dock, taking its name either from the surname of the owner or from the fact that it was used as a watering place for horses. The name is mentioned by Ben Jonson in *Bartholomew Fair*. Dean Swift has a Countess of Puddle Dock in *Polite Conversation* and William Hogarth introduced a Duke of Puddle Dock in his *Trip to Gravesend*. The name also became synonymous with low life and criminal activities.

*The statue of Queen
Anne in Queen
Anne's Gate*

Pump Court, EC4
Here stood the pump
from which the local
inhabitants drew their
water.

**Queen Anne's Gate,
SW1**
Built as two separate closes in the early eighteenth century, it was
turned into one street in 1873, when the dividing wall was taken
down. The 'new' street is dominated by the statue of Queen Anne,
whose name it bears.

Queen Elizabeth's Walk, N16
Tradition, rather than fact, records that Elizabeth I had a country seat
here in the sixteenth century.

Queenhithe, EC4
The street leads to one of the oldest docks on the river – a hithe being
an inlet in the bank where ships could be unloaded. The name first
appears in a charter of King Alfred, dated 899, and the dock came
under royal patronage in the twelfth century.

Queen's Gate, SW7
Named after the gate into the royal Hyde Park, the street forms the
boundary between Kensington and Westminster.

Queen Square, WC1
Named after Queen Anne, although originally called Devonshire Square.

Queen Street, EC4
Named in honour of Charles II's queen, Catharine of Braganza, the street was made after the Great Fire and formed a direct route from the Guildhall to the river.

Queensway, W2
Originally called Black Horse Lane, this was renamed after Queen Victoria, who used to go riding there when she lived at Kensington Palace.

Queen Victoria Street, EC4
The street was built as part of a road-improvement scheme in the nineteenth century which involved cutting several new streets to ease traffic congestion. Previously this area was a maze of small streets and alleys.

Railway Place, EC3
This is so called from its proximity to Fenchurch Street station, the only mainline terminus wholly within the City of London.

Rainsford Street, W2
It commemorates the Reverend Marcus Rainsford, vicar of St James's, Sussex Gardens, 1904-31.

Queen's Gate

Ramillies Street, W1
The defeat of the French by the Duke of Marlborough in Flanders in 1706 is remembered here.

Rampayne Street, SW1
In 1705 Charles Rampayne set up a fund by which the children of the Grey Coat Hospital could be apprenticed. Under the title of Westminster Technical Fund this grant is still awarded today.

Ram Place, E9
In 1723 a nonconformist chapel was built here by a certain Stephen Ram – hence Ram's Chapel.

Ranelagh Gardens, SW3
Now part of the grounds of the Royal Hospital, Chelsea, the gardens were a highly fashionable place in the eighteenth century. Paymaster at the time of William and Mary, Lord Ranelagh built himself a grand house here 'at public expense'.

Rectory Grove, SW4
It leads from the Old Town, with Clapham's parish church of St Paul, to the 'new' town around the common. The home of the Rector of Clapham formerly stood here.

Rede Place, W2
Richard Rede was granted the manor of Paddington by Henry VIII at the time of the dissolution of the monasteries. The family held the manor until the 1620s.

Red Lion Square, WC1
Developed by Dr Nicholas Barbon in the seventeenth century, it takes its name from a nearby tavern.

Regent Street, W1
The street was laid out by John Nash, the favourite architect of the Prince Regent, later George IV, as part of his plan to create a royal processional way from Carlton House (where Carlton House Terrace now stands) to the newly designed (but never built) Regent's Palace in what was then Marylebone Park.

Rex Place, W1
Until 1951 this street was shown as King's Mews, then it was changed to *Rex*, the Latin for king. History does not record if there

was a particular king to be remembered here. Perhaps the space on the map was too small to fit one in!

Richmond Terrace, SW1
Built between 1822 and 1825 to the design of Thomas Chawner, it replaced Richmond House, which had been designed by the Earl of Burlington for Charles, second Duke of Richmond.

Ridley Road, E7 and E8
Ownership of the local manor was vested in the Bishops of London. Nicholas Ridley, Bishop 1550-3, was the last to hold it before it reverted to the crown.

Ring Cross, N1
At the junction of Liverpool Road and Holloway Road there once stood a gibbet for the execution of criminals – at the crossroads.

Robert Street, WC2
Robert Adam (1728-92) was the best known of the Adam brothers and the architect of many stately homes.

Rochester Row, SW1
The Bishops of Rochester had a house here from 1666 to the early nineteenth century.

Rolls Buildings, Rolls Passage, EC4
The name derives from the practice of keeping documents in rolls inside pipes which were housed here. The site was once occupied by the house of maintenance for converted Jews and the chapel forms part of the Public Records Office today.

Romilly Street, W1
Sir Samuel Romilly (1757-1818), the advocate and law-reformer, was one of many legal men who lived in Holborn – first in Gower Street and subsequently in Russell Square.

Ronalds Road, N5
One of the pioneers of the electric telegraph, Sir Francis Ronalds (1788-1873), lived here.

Rood Lane, EC3
Beside the church of St Margaret Pattens, the lane recalls either the setting up here, in medieval times, of a large rood (cross) in the churchyard, or that roods and other religious items were made here.

Rookery Road, SW4
Clapham Common today is a vast expanse of grass, with playing areas for all to enjoy, but in past times the scene was much more rural, with trees in which rooks built their nests.

Ropemaker Street, EC1
In the large open space outside the City wall ropemakers would ply their trade and the area became a ropewalk for making ropes.

Rose Alley, SE1
The office development here and in Park Street is built over the excavation of the Elizabethan Rose Theatre. At the time of William Shakespeare there were theatres, such as the Globe, along Bankside in the liberty of the Clink. Although the theatre in Shoreditch was London's first, the Rose Theatre, built near a house of that name, was the forerunner of all those in Southwark, having been built about 1587.

Rosoman Street, EC1
When it was first shown on maps the street was called Bridewell Walk, passing as it did the Clerkenwell bridewell (prison). In 1756, when the builder Rosoman rebuilt the nearby Sadlers Wells Theatre, he also built a terrace of houses and named them after himself.

Rosslyn Hill, NW3
Formerly called Red Lion Hill after the public house which stood where the police station now stands, the name now recalls the Earls of Rosslyn who lived in the area during the eighteenth century.

Rotten Row, Hyde Park, SW1 and SW7
Sometimes shown as *rotteran*, meaning 'to muster', it might have been used as a mustering ground in the English Civil War, or it may derive from the king's way (*rue de roi*) from Westminster and Whitehall to Kensington Palace and Hampton Court.

Roupell Street, SE1
A member of the local vestry, William Roupell was elected member of parliament by the then extraordinary majority of 9318 votes. His election figures caused such a commotion that a select committee was set up to investigate, but he was exonerated.

Rowe Lane, E9
After his death in 1661 Owen Rowe, one of the judges of Charles I, was buried in the churchyard of St John's, Hackney.

Rowland Hill Street, NW3
Running between two hospitals, the street commemorates the man who in 1840 established the uniform Penny Post – any letter anywhere for one penny.

Sir Rowland Hill

Royal Arcade, off Old Bond Street, W1
This shopping street was granted royal status after a visit from Queen Victoria.

Royal Avenue, intended by Wren to link the Royal Hospital at Chelsea with Kensington Palace

Royal Avenue, SW3
Stately boulevards are rare in London but here at least is the start of one, designed by Sir Christopher Wren to link his Royal Hospital at Chelsea with the rebuilt Nottingham House – Kensington Palace – for William III. It was completed in 1694, but the terrace houses were added in the early nineteenth century.

Royal Hospital Road, SW3
On the site of a former monastic almshouse, theological college and military prison, Charles II built, it is said at the instigation of Nell Gwynne, an infirmary or college of residence for retired soldiers. The Royal Hospital can accommodate up to four hundred veteran soldiers.

Royal Opera Arcade, SW1
Her Majesty's Theatre, Haymarket, was built in 1705 as an opera house. When John Nash rebuilt it in 1818 he replaced the former dressing and green rooms with a colonnade of shops.

Russell Square, WC1; Russell Street, WC2
This part of the estate of the Dukes of Bedford, whose family name is Russell, was given to them in the seventeenth century. Russell

Square is the third largest in London, being surpassed only by Grosvenor Square and Lincoln's Inn Fields.

Sackville Street, W1

It is said that while he was building St James's church, Piccadilly, Sir Christopher Wren laid out some of the nearby streets. One of the first families to move in here was that of Edward Sackville, a younger brother of the Earl of Dorset. An unusual feature of the street is that it has no side turnings and is the longest street in the West End so conceived.

Saffron Hill, EC1

Gardens abounded in medieval London and one of the finest belonged to the Bishops of Ely, whose land covered a wide area just outside the City wall. The Bishop's diocese included Saffron Walden, Essex, from where his gardeners brought saffron or yellow crocus.

St Albans Road, NW5

After her first husband, the banker Thomas Coutts, died, the actress Helen Mellom married the ninth Duke of St Albans. On her death in 1827 she left the Holly Hill estate, Highgate, to Thomas Coutts's grand-daughter, Angela Burdett.

St Albans Street, SW1

Charles II granted a parcel of land here to Henry Jermyn, Earl of St Albans, in 1661.

St Alphonsus Road, SW4

The Catholic Order of Redemptionists was founded by St Alphonsus, whose monastery stands here.

St Andrew Street, EC4

The street leads to and from the parish church of St Andrew Holborn whose rectory and courthouse were built to the designs of S. S. Teulon.

St Anselms Place, W1

From 1896 to 1988 a church dedicated to St Anselm, the Benedictine Abbot of Bec and Archbishop of Canterbury, stood here. It replaced the Hanover Chapel in Regent Street.

St Barnabas Street, SW11

Consecrated in 1850 by Dr Charles Blomfield, Bishop of London, as a chapel of ease to St Paul's, Knightsbridge, the church of St Barnabas was the scene of a number of protests as a centre of the ritualistic movement of the nineteenth century.

St Chad's Place, WC1
This was the site of St Chad's holy well, whose medicinal waters were often used for their professed healing properties.

St Clare Street, EC3; St Clare Place, E1
A follower of St Francis of Assisi, St Clare founded the 'Poor Clares' or 'Minoresses', whose London home was here in the middle ages.

St Dunstan's Lane, St Dunstan's Hill, EC3
As early as the thirteenth century there was a church here dedicated to St Dunstan. It is often given the suffix 'in-the-East' to differentiate it from St Dunstan's-in-the-West in Fleet Street.

St Ermin's Hill, off Broadway, SW1
Records show in the sixteenth century a chapel dedicated to St Armil (or Ermil) here when Van Dun built almshouses on land 'leading up to the chapel of...' It is likely that, during his exile in Britanny, Henry VII visited the monastery of St Armel des Boschaux and became devoted to him. Traditionally the king is said to have believed that the saint was responsible for his becoming King of England. This is borne out by the fact that there are two statues of the saint in Henry VII's Chapel in Westminster Abbey.

St George's Fields, Bayswater Road, W2
The housing estate is built on the site of the former burial ground of the parish of St George's, Hanover Square.

St George's Lane, EC3
One of the few churches dedicated to the patron saint of England was founded here in the thirteenth century. It was demolished in 1904.

St George Street, W1
This is a polite gesture to honour George I, during whose reign this part of London was developed, rather than the patron saint of England.

St Giles High Street, WC2
One of the lost villages of London, St Giles's once contained a lepers' hospital founded by Queen Matilda in 1101. The High Street, the centre of the village's life, today acts as a tributary to busy London traffic.

St Helena Street, WC1
The street dates from the time of Napoleon's death in 1821. The site had previously been occupied by pleasure grounds of St Helena's Gardens.

St Helen's Place, Great St Helen's, EC3
Unique among the many churches of the City in its dedication, St Helen's was founded in the twelfth century as a Benedictine nunnery and a parish church. St Helen was the Emperor Constantine's mother and 'finder of the True Cross on which Christ was crucified'.

St James's Square, SW1
North of Pall Mall, the square was laid out during the second half of the seventeenth century by Henry Jermyn, first Earl of St Albans. There are a number of interesting houses in the square, including Norfolk House, rebuilt in 1939, and used by General Eisenhower when he was superintending the invasions of Europe and North Africa during the Second World War.

St James's Street, SW1
A lazar (leper) house run by fourteen chaste maidens was founded here in the twelfth century and continued in use as a hospice until the dissolution of the monasteries in the sixteenth century. Dedicated to St James the Less, it stood where St James's Palace is today. In Strype's time, the eighteenth century, the street is described as being 'spacious with some houses having a terrace walk'. The street was the first in London to have a road-island for the benefit of pedestrians wishing to cross the road; the island was made in 1864 at the instigation of an army colonel who found the traffic too difficult to negotiate when leaving his club in the street. It was also in this street, when it was known as Long Street, that in 1670 Colonel Blood made his desperate attempt on the life of the Duke of Ormonde, even though he was guarded by six footmen. The Duke was dragged from his coach and pulled towards Tyburn (Marble Arch of today), where his assailants intended to hang him from the notorious gallows. The villains were chased and, although they escaped, the Duke was rescued, being found struggling in the mud in Piccadilly.

St John's Hill, SW11
The lords of the manor of Battersea were the Viscounts Bolingbroke, whose family name was St John.

St John's Street, St John's Square, St John's Lane, EC1
Just outside the City wall the Order of the Hospital of St John of Jerusalem founded their London house in 1144.

St Katherine's Way, E1
This runs along the boundary of the former St Katherine's Dock,

*St John's
Gateway in
Clerkenwell*

which in turn was named after St Katherine's Hospital, a charitable foundation founded by the consort of King Stephen, Queen Matilda, in 1148.

St Loo Avenue, SW3
This was named after the sixteenth-century lady better known as Bess of Hardwick, builder of houses. Her fourth (and last) husband was the Earl of Shrewsbury; Bess's titles included Lady St Loo, Countess of Shrewsbury. Shrewsbury House was in Cheyne Walk.

St Margaret Street, SW1
While Westminster Abbey might be considered the royal church for the nearby royal palace, both palace and abbey owing their existence to King Edward the Confessor, St Margaret's church is for the people of Westminster and is also the parish church for both Houses of Parliament.

St Martin's Close, NW1

Bought in 1803 to provide extra burial ground for the parish of St Martin's in the Fields, Trafalgar Square, the Close was built on an unused portion of the four-acre site. Originally the site was occupied by almshouses for the poor of St Martin's. They still stand in nearby Bayham Street.

St Martin's Lane, WC2

One of the oldest thoroughfares in the parish of St Martin's in the Fields, the lane was first laid out, as West Church Lane, in 1613.

St Martin's-le-Grand, EC1

In the sixteenth century Protector Somerset required stone to build himself a new house in the Strand – Somerset House. He acquired the stone from the Benedictine monastery dedicated to St Martin in the City. The name first appears on maps in 1265 and remains today as a memory of London's monastic past.

St Mary at Hill, EC3

Church and street share the same name, with the suffix 'at Hill' coming from the steep ascent from Billingsgate. Stow says that Thomas Becket, later Archbishop of Canterbury, was a priest here.

St Mary Axe, EC3

In 1561 the dilapidated parish church of St Mary Axe was demolished and the parish amalgamated with St Andrew Undershaft. At this time an axe, said to have been the one used to martyr St Ursula and her virgins, was removed from the church and ordered to be destroyed as being idolatrous.

St Matthew Street, SW1

Improvements in the middle of the nineteenth century, such as the making of Victoria Street and the clearing away of the slums in the area, led to the disappearance of a number of streets and alleys. Duck Lane, a notorious place by all accounts, was replaced by a street named after the new local church built to the designs of Sir Gilbert Scott in 1840.

St Michael's Alley, EC3

The church of St Michael at one end of the alley was founded in Saxon times and in 1055 was given to the Abbey of Evesham.

St Michael's Street, W2

From 1860 to 1966 the main entrance to the church dedicated to the Archangel Michael was in this street. Bombed in the Second

World War, it was finally pulled down in 1966. The street was previously known as Market Street when it served the needs of the bargees of the nearby canal.

St Mildred's Court, EC2
The church dedicated to St Mildred was demolished in 1872. In the painting 'The Cellist' by I. J. H. Bradley (1832) in the Phillips Collection, Washington DC, the music on the piano is entitled *Mildred Court*.

St Paul's Road, N1
St Paul's church was built in 1828 to the designs of Sir Charles Barry. Previously the road was shown on maps as Hopping Lane, from a local hop ground.

St Peter's Alley, off Cornhill, EC3
This public right of way circumnavigates part of the churchyard of the site of the oldest Christian church in the City of London, St Peter-upon-Cornhill.

St Petersburg Place, W2
Visits from the heads of state of other nations are noted in various London street names. Peter the Great, Tsar of Russia, stayed in Paddington while studying naval architecture, but this street was named in honour of Tsar Alexander, who came here after the Napoleonic wars.

St Philip's Place, W2
The building erected in 1854 as a temporary place of Christian worship survived until 1894, by which time it had become fully recognised.

St Swithin's Lane, EC4
The church of St Swithin was a victim of the Blitz during the Second World War and it has been replaced by the Bank of China.

Sale Place, W2
One of the many engineers involved in the building of the Grand Junction Canal, Richard Cowlishaw Sale, is commemorated here.

Salisbury Square, Salisbury Court, EC4
Once the site of one of the London homes of the Bishops of Salisbury, it was later occupied by the Sackville family. Here, too, Samuel Richardson wrote *Pamela* and set up his printing press. To encourage his staff to arrive at work on time and to keep busy he used to hide a half-crown in the type, thereby ensuring that the first man in would have a better chance of earning a bonus.

Salters Hall Court, EC4
Here, on the site of the house of Henry Fitzalwyn, the first Mayor of London, the Worshipful Company of Salters first set up their hall in 1641. It was rebuilt in 1827 but destroyed in the Second World War by enemy action.

Sans Walk, EC1
In 1893 the oldest member of the parish vestry of St John and St James was honoured by having this walk named after him.

Sardinia Street, WC2
Completely rebuilt between 1901 and 1905, with the development of Kingsway and Aldwych, the street commemorates the Sardinian embassy, which stood here. The chapel was staffed by Roman Catholic Franciscans, who attracted a staunch congregation of believers in the 'Old Faith'. Consequently the embassy was attacked by mobs in the 'No Popery' riots of 1780-1.

Savile Row, W1
Richard, Earl of Burlington and Cork, married Dorothy, daughter of George Savile, Earl of Halifax, who owned land in this neighbourhood until early in the eighteenth century.

Savoy Place, Savoy Street, Savoy Hill, Savoy Court, WC2
One of the royal palaces around London was the Savoy Palace, originally built on the riverside along The Strand by Peter, Count of Savoy, on a site granted by Henry III in 1245. Later John of Gaunt rebuilt the palace and its private chapel, the Chapel Royal.

Scout Lane, SW4
A lane that once led to Grove House today leads to the headquarters of the Fifth Clapham BP Scout Company.

Sedley Place, W1
An act of sheer cheek gives this place its name. In 1873 one Angelo Sedley set up a furniture store here. He then asked permission, and got it, to name the place after himself.

Seething Lane, EC3
Near the lane was a corn market and the chaff from it must have blown across this part of the City. The Old English word for chaff was *ceafen* and through the years the present name has evolved.

Serjeant's Inn, off 49 Fleet Street, EC4
Although the title and office of the Serjeants at Law has disap-

peared from the courts, the site of their inn remains.

Sermon Lane, EC4
The preaching of sermons in the open air was a common event in the middle ages, and when there was a convenient place to preach one on the processional path around the precincts of the cathedral it is hardly surprising that it became a regular stop.

Seven Dials, WC2
Speculative builder Thomas Neale built a series of seven streets radiating from a circus. In the middle he erected a Doric column capped with seven faces (dials). The column was later removed to Weybridge in Surrey but a new 40 foot (12 metre) column was unveiled by Queen Beatrix of the Netherlands on 28th June 1989.

Seven Sisters Road, N4, N7 and N15
King Robert Bruce of Scotland had seven daughters, each of whom planted an elm tree here, so the road became known as the Seven Sisters from the daughters and the trees.

Shaftesbury Avenue, W1 and WC2
Standing in the centre of Piccadilly Circus is a statue wrongly described as Eros, the God of Love. It is, in fact, the Shaftesbury Memorial and the figure on top is a rebus to Lord Shaftesbury, the nineteenth-century philanthropist after whom the street is named. The figure is shooting a shaft (arrow) into the earth, thereby burying it.

Shaver's Place (leading from Coventry Street to Haymarket), SW1
The Earl of Pembroke's barber set up his shop here after the nearby Spring Gardens, a pleasure place, was demolished.

Sheldon Street, W2
Gilbert Sheldon, Bishop of London and Lord of the Manor of Paddington, leased the land to his nephews, one of whom, Sir Joseph Sheldon, became Lord Mayor of London in 1676.

Shepherd Market, Shepherd Street, Shepherd's Place, W1
Edward Shepherd bought much of the land where the May Fair was held from medieval times until the seventeenth century, and he developed the site into a residential area.

Sheraton Street, W1
Before parts of Soho acquired a reputation as the headquarters for the British film industry it was well-known for the production of

high-class furniture. Here came Thomas Sheraton in the late eighteenth century.

Sherlock Mews, W1
Sir Arthur Conan Doyle's fictional detective, who 'lived' at 221B Baker Street, is commemorated here.

Shoe Lane, EC4
In the thirteenth century there is mention of a 'Showell Lane in the parish of St Andrewe Holebourne' as being a gathering point for apprentices on holy days. There is an alternative suggestion that the lane led to a field shaped like a shoe.

Shooters Hill, SE18
It is possible that archers gathered here in the middle ages to practise their skill. Alternatively coaches, after the long climb up the hill, may suddenly have shot over the top.

Shore Place, Shore Road, E9
Jane Shore, the mistress of Edward IV and the wife of a London goldsmith, William Shore, was accused by Richard III of witchcraft. She was found guilty by an ecclesiastical court and made to walk with a taper in her hand through the streets of London.

Siddons Lane, NW1
One of the great actresses of the English theatre, Sarah Siddons retired

The statue of Sarah Siddons on Paddington Green

from the stage in 1817 and, apart from a short time when she lived in Paddington, spent the rest of her life in Upper Baker Street.

Sise Lane, EC4
The name is abbreviated from St Osyth, who, according to legend built a nunnery at Chick in Essex. Marauding Danes one day seized and beheaded her but, after they had left, Osyth picked herself up, including her head, and walked into the church at Chick. The nuns, fearing more raids by the Danes, transferred her body to Aylesbury, but she once again rose up and demanded to be buried at Chick. This was done and she now rests safely at St Osyth in Essex. She was remembered in London by a church dedicated to her, which was later destroyed in the Great Fire and not rebuilt.

Sloane Street, Sloane Square, SW1
After his retirement in 1742, Sir Hans Sloane, the noted physician and collector, bought the manor house in Chelsea and there he lived and later died.

Smithfield, EC1
The 'smoothfield' outside the City wall was where apprentices and others used to practise the ancient arts of warfare. From early in the twelfth century it was regularly used to hold fairs and other events, in particular the Bartholomew Fair, which survived until 1855. Today the whole of one side is taken up by the Smithfield Meat Market, built by Sir Horace Jones between 1862 and 1865.

Snow Hill, EC1
A Scandinavian trader, Snorro, lived here, and in Stow's time it was known as Snore Hill. By the time John Bunyan died in 1688 'at the sign of the Star on Snow Hill' it had acquired its present name.

Soho Square, W1
Originally laid out in 1681 by Gregory King and named after him, it takes its present title from the area which it serves so well today. Before being built on, the fields here were used for hunting and the cries 'so-so' or 'so-ho', the English equivalents of the French 'tally-ho', filled the air. During the Battle of Sedgemoor in 1685, the last major battle fought on English soil, the Duke of Monmouth, whose house filled the south side of the square, used 'Soho' as a password.

115

Soho Square

Southampton Buildings, WC2
This was part of the estate of Lord Southampton, which was developed in the early seventeenth century.

Southampton Street, WC2
The street was dominated by Bedford House, the home of the Russells, Dukes of Bedford, until its demolition in 1704. The wife of Lord William Russell was the daughter of the Earl of Southampton.

Southwark
The South Ward of the City of London, outside the City wall, it was not officially part of the City until 1550 when the Lord Mayor, Sir Rowland Hill, rode round the area proclaiming it to be 'now under the jurisdiction of the City of London'.

South Wharf Road, W2
Along the south side of the Paddington basin of the Grand Junction Canal barges were loaded and unloaded when the canal was in full use.

Spaniards Road, NW3
This road, which crosses Hampstead Heath, leads to the Spaniards Inn, which is said to have acquired its name either from two Spaniards who kept the inn in the eighteenth century or because it was once lived in by a Spanish ambassador to the Court of St James's.

Spital Square, E1
Founded in 1197 by Walter and Rosia Brune, the priory of St Mary Spital was a hospital for mentally disturbed patients.

Spring Gardens, SW1
This part of London was once the King's property, being part of the grounds of Whitehall Palace. Here there were sites for practising archery and bathing places for the courtiers. To discourage trespassers a device was hidden among the steps so that a jet of water sprang up into the face of anyone walking on them – hence the name.

Spring Mews, W1
This was so called from a pond called Spring Pond that was fed by a spring nearby.

Spring Street, W2
There are numerous springs in the vicinity, including one under Trinity Court, Bishop's Bridge Road.

Spring Gardens, named after the water jets concealed here

Spurstowe Road, Spurstowe Terrace, E8

In the seventeenth century a parish benefactor and vicar of Hackney by the name of Spurstowe left lands for the poor on which were built the Spurstowe Almshouses.

Stable Yard, SW1

Close by Lancaster House the stable arcade was rebuilt by Nicholas Hawksmoor between 1716 and 1717.

Stafford Street, W1

In the Duke of Albemarle public house on the corner of the street there is a tablet reading 'This is Stafford Street, 1686'. The name remembers Margaret Stafford, who was a partner of Sir Thomas Bond in his development of the land in the seventeenth century.

Stag Place, SW1

The Stag Brewery, demolished in 1959, was the successor of the old brewhouse and baking house of Westminster Abbey. It moved here after the dissolution of the monasteries in the sixteenth century. The original post-dissolution brewers were Greenes and they were succeeded by Watneys, part of whose arms was a stag rampant.

Staple Inn Buildings, WC1

The inn is believed to have been originally a wool market or a hostel for the wool merchants (staplers). In the fifteenth century it became an inn of Chancery, later passing into the ownership of Gray's Inn opposite.

Star Street, W2

It is assumed that in the nineteenth century there was a public house here but the records are blank on the subject.

Stationers' Hall Court, EC4

The Worshipful Company of Stationers used to enjoy a monopoly of printing all books, and books 'entered at Stationers' Hall' were protected by a primitive form of copyright. The company's hall was rebuilt here, after the Great Fire.

Steele's Road, Steele's Mews, NW3

Sir Richard Steele (1672-1729), the author, lived in a small cottage on Haverstock Hill.

Stoke Newington
Dating from the Saxon period, the name means a new town (ton) in or near a wood, although as 'a clearing in the wood' it is said to date from much earlier.

Stonhouse Street, SW4
An absentee rector of Clapham, Sir James Stonhouse, Baronet, preferred to live in Oxfordshire on his family estate rather than to perform his clerical duties in London.

Storey's Gate, SW1
Keeper of the aviary in Birdcage Walk, Edward Storey lived here in the time of Charles II.

The Strand, WC2
This road connecting Charing Cross with the City originally ran near the riverbank (strand) and appears on maps as early as 1245.

Stratford Place, W1
This cul-de-sac leading off Oxford Street terminates with Stratford House, built about 1774 by Lord Stratford and others.

Stratton Street, W1
Sir John Berkeley, later Lord Berkeley of Stratton, was the hero of the Royalist victory at Stratton, Cornwall, in 1643. The street was later built on land he owned.

Strutton Ground, SW1
Lord Dacre's house stood here in the sixteenth century but has long since disappeared. The site was known as Stourton Meadow before the house was built.

Strype Street, E1
This was formerly shown as Strype's Yard, from the fact that John Strype, a silk merchant, lived here.

Stukeley Street, WC2
The rector of St George's church, Bloomsbury, between 1747 and 1765 was the Reverend William Stukeley, the antiquarian known also as 'the Arch Druid'. He is still remembered in this street name.

Suffolk Lane, EC4
The Dukes of Suffolk lived here in splendid mansions whose gardens stretched down to the river.

Suffolk Street, SW1
One of the original streets formed in 1664 on the site where once
the Earls of Suffolk had a town house of some significance.

Summerhouse Road, N16
Here stood a summerhouse, in the grounds of Mr John Wilmer, an
eccentric Quaker who died in 1764 leaving instructions in his will
that he should be buried in the garden. He also left money for the
upkeep of a bell-pull from his grave to the house.

Surrey Street, WC2
Built on land owned by the Howard family which, through one of
its branches, held the earldoms of Arundel and Surrey.

Sussex Gardens, Sussex Place, Sussex Square, W2
Ever popular with those who name streets, royal dukes are remembered in a number of places in London. Much of the estate in this
southern portion of Paddington was begun in 1843, the year of the
death of George III's sixth son, the Duke of Sussex, but the
Gardens were originally called Grand Junction Road, and the
houses on either side Cambridge Terrace and Oxford Terrace. It
was renamed in 1936.

Sutton Court Road, W4
Sutton Court here in Chiswick was the home of the Earl and
Countess Falconberg in the seventeenth century. Lady Falconberg
was Oliver Cromwell's third daughter.

Sutton Place, E9
Thomas Sutton was a lawyer who had a passion for travelling. On
returning from his continental tour in the sixteenth century he
became Elizabeth I's Master of the Ordnance and sailed his own
ship against the Armada of 1588. Afterwards he settled in Homerton
and furnished his house, it is said, with items from the battle. He
retired to Charterhouse, where he set up a home for retired men.

Sutton Row, W1
Here was the town house of Thomas, Lord Falconberg, who mar-
ried a daughter of Oliver Cromwell. Their country house at
Chiswick was Sutton Court.

Swan Walk, SW3
All swans on the Thames belong to the Queen, except those whose
beaks have been 'nicked' by the Dyers' and Vintners' companies

by ancient privilege in the swan-upping ceremony.

Tadema Road, SW10
The Dutch-born doctor turned painter Alma-Tadema came to England in 1870 and settled in Chelsea.

Templar Road, E9
This is a reminder of the ownership of land here by the Knights Templars, one of the two great military monastic orders of the middle ages.

Temple, EC4
The Knights Templars of St John of Jerusalem set up their first London home where now Southampton Buildings are, at the northern end of Chancery Lane. Then, in the twelfth century, they acquired land between Fleet Street and the river. Early in the fourteenth century they were disbanded and the ground was transferred to the Knights Hospitallers who leased the ground to lawyers. In a perpetual lease of 1608 in the reign of James I, lawyers were granted the freehold of the Inner and Middle Temple. The outer Temple was sold separately and was later developed into residential property.

Temple Mills Road, E15
Three waterwheels in the river Lea were probably the earliest industry in the area.

Tenter Street, EC2
The street was occupied for over two hundred years by Dutch Jews in exile from Holland. Here, in the open space outside the City wall, the cloth workers had their tenters or stretching frames.

Thaives Lane, EC4
John Thaive, an armourer in Edward III's time, lived here and after his death in 1348 his estate became an inn of Chancery belonging to Lincoln's Inn.

Thames Street, Lower EC3, Upper EC4
The longest street in the City, reaching from the Tower of London in the east to Blackfriars in the west, it runs by the river Thames.

Theobalds Road, WC1
Kings and queens of England travelling to their palace at Theobalds in Hertfordshire went along this country lane which has now become a busy thoroughfare.

Thomas More Street, E1
Henry VIII's former Lord Chancellor Thomas More refused to acknowledge the legality of the king's divorce from Catherine of Aragon and his marriage to Anne Boleyn, and this led to his execution on Tower Hill in 1535. Thomas More was canonised by the Roman Catholic Church in 1935.

Threadneedle Street, EC2
In earlier days the street is shown as Three Needles Street, either from the fact that the Needlemakers' Company had their hall here (their coat of arms includes three needles), or from the Merchant Taylors, whose hall has been here since the fourteenth century.

Three Kings Yard, W1
Until 1879, when it was demolished, there was a tavern called Three Kings at the entrance.

Throgmorton Avenue, Throgmorton Street, EC2
Sir Nicholas Throgmorton, ambassador to France at the time of Elizabeth I, is buried in the church of St Katharine Cree.

Thurlow Park Road, SE21
In about 1780 Lord Thurlow, the Lord Chancellor, lived in Dulwich while an old farmhouse on Knights Hill was being converted into a stately home for him.

Tite Street, SW3
For his work in connection with the Chelsea Embankment in the latter half of the nineteenth century Sir William Tite is commemorated here.

Throgmorton Avenue and Drapers' Hall

Tokenhouse Yard, EC2

A mint house stood here before the accession of James I to the English throne. It was used for making farthing tokens when silver pennies were the smallest coins of the realm.

Tollington Park, Tollington Place, N4; Tollington Road, Tollington Way, N7

Anglo-Saxon charters show this area as being called *Tollandune*, meaning 'the hill or hill pasture of Tolla'. The name is spelt *Totenstone* in the Domesday Survey of 1086.

Tothill Street, SW1

In the King James I Bible, the Second Book of Samuel describes how David took the *stronghold* of Zion, but Wycliffe translated the word as *totehill*. The gatehouse prison stood at the Victoria Street end and in it such notable men as Sir Walter Raleigh, the dwarf Sir Jeffery Hudson and Samuel Pepys were imprisoned.

Tottenham Court Road, W1

In existence in the twelfth century, the road led from the village of St Giles in the Fields to the prebendal manor of Toten or Ten Hale, which is mentioned in the Domesday Survey of 1086. William de Totenhale had a mansion at the north end of the road.

Tradescant Road, SW8

Gardener to Charles I and Robert Cecil of Hatfield House, John Tradescant lived in Lambeth and is buried in the graveyard of the former parish church, now the Museum of Garden History. He introduced plants to this country from Virginia.

Trafalgar Square, WC2 and SW1

There was nothing distinguished about the area until well into the nineteenth century when the Charing Cross Improvement Bill of 1826 set out to improve the whole district around the former King's Mews. It was William IV who suggested that the square should be used as a memorial to Lord Nelson and that it should be called Trafalgar after his greatest and last sea victory.

Tresham Avenue, E9

A grand prior of the Order of St John, Sir Thomas Tresham bought land in Hackney at the dissolution of the Order of Knights Templars.

Trafalgar Square and the Christmas tree annually given by the people of Norway

Trevor Square, SW7
Sir John Trevor, Speaker of the House of Commons, lived here in the eighteenth century.

Tudor Street, EC4
Passing through the area of Whitefriars, which later became 'Alsatia', a notorious sanctuary for thieves and vagabonds, Tudor Street terminates in New Bridge Street. At the dissolution of the monastic establishments here, the area became a fashionable place in which to live. The Tudor king, Henry VIII, built himself a palace here – Bridewell. Later the palace was made over to the City and used as a poorhouse and prison.

Tufton Street, SW1
In this area the monks of Westminster Abbey had a bowling alley. The street was built in the seventeenth century, originally for Sir Richard Tufton, who lived here and who is buried in the abbey.

Turnmill Street, EC1
There were so many mills beside the river Fleet that a stretch of it

was often called the Turnmill Brook, and the name survives in this street which lies alongside the river.

Turnstile, Great and Little, WC1
The narrow lanes leading out of Lincoln's Inn Fields and towards Holborn were once guarded by turnstiles to prevent cattle from straying away from the Fields.

Tyburn Way, W1
On the road-island opposite the Odeon cinema, Marble Arch, is a plaque commemorating the site of Tyburn Tree, a gallows last used in 1783 for the hanging of John Austin. It stood twelve feet high, was triangular in shape and was capable of hanging eight people on each of its three sides.

Tyssen Road, N16
Over the years London has played host to immigrants of many different nationalities. A Dutch family who became wealthy land-owners in the district were the Tyssens.

Udall Street, SW1
Nicholas Udall, sixteenth-century dramatist and scholar, was head-master of Eton and of Westminster School and the author of *Ralph Roister Doister*, the earliest known English comedy.

Undershaft, EC3
This was named for the maypole that used to stand in Leadenhall Street until Evil May Day in 1517, when it was torn down and destroyed. The nearby church is known as St Andrew Undershaft for the same reason.

Urswick Road, E9
The ending of the Wars of the Roses between the houses of York and Lancaster was signified by the marriage of the victor of Bosworth, Henry VII, and Elizabeth of York. The marriage treaty was negotiated by Christopher Urswick, later Rector of Hackney from 1502 to 1522.

Vane Street, SW1
Sir Harry Vane, Puritan and prominent Parliamentarian, was a pupil at Westminster School. Already unpopular with monarchists and by 1659 distrusted by all his own parties, after the Restoration of the Monarchy in 1660 he was tried, found guilty of high treason and executed.

Venables Street, NW8
This street is named after the Rector of Christ Church, Bell Street, the Reverend Edward Venables, who died in 1891.

Venn Street, SW4
Born in Clapham in the mid eighteenth century when his father was curate there, later rector there himself, John Venn was a member of the Clapham Sect, a group dedicated to the abolition of slavery in the British Empire.

Vere Street, W1
Named after Aubrey de Vere (died 1703), the twentieth and last of the de Veres, Earls of Oxford, landlords here.

Victoria Embankment, EC4, WC2 and SW1
Begun in 1864 and completed in 1870, the Embankment was designed by Sir Joseph Bazalgette and dedicated in honour of Queen Victoria, the reigning monarch.

Victoria Tower Gardens, SW1
After the destruction by fire of the old Palace of St Stephen at Westminster in 1834, it was rebuilt to the designs of Sir Charles Barry. At each end of the palace is a tower; one houses the great

Victoria Embankment

bell known as Big Ben, after the then Commissioner of Works, Sir Benjamin Hall, and the other is the Victoria Tower, which is used today to house documents relating to both Houses of Parliament.

Vigo Street, W1
Shortly after the victory of the British and Dutch fleets over the French off Vigo in Spain in 1702 the name of Vigo Lane appears on maps of London. This later became Vigo Street.

Villiers Street, WC2
Occupying part of the site of York House, the street was laid out in 1674-5 as part of a development scheme carried out by George Villiers, Duke of Buckingham.

Vincent Square, SW1
William Vincent was Dean of Westminster from 1802 to 1815. The square, which occupies part of the old Tothill Fields, was made into playing fields for the boys of Westminster School during his period of office.

Vine Street, W1
There are several streets in the London area with this name and each of them is considered to have been so called because there were formerly vineyards in the neighbourhood.

Vintners Place, EC4
It follows the line of the walls of the Worshipful Company of Vintners' Hall and leads down to the riverside, where wines were unloaded in medieval times.

Waithman Street, EC4
Robert Waithman, Lord Mayor of London in 1823, guarded the body of George IV's Queen Caroline on its journey to the coast. She was buried in Brunswick.

Walbrook, EC4
Running from beside the Mansion House to Cannon Street, the street takes its name from one of London's lost rivers, the Walbrook, which rises in the fields north of the City, crosses the City wall by Moorgate and then runs southwards to enter the Thames at Dowgate.

Wapping Stairs, E1
Originally the home of the Waepping or Eapping family, Wapping is first recorded in the year 1230.

Wardour Street, W1

Henry, Lord Arundel of Wardour, the landlord, developed this and the surrounding streets.

Wardrobe Court, off Carter Lane, EC4

Away from the hustle and bustle of the City's traffic, the court marks the site of the house bought by Edward III for storing the royal state robes. Pepys visited the house several times to call upon his cousin, the Earl of Sandwich, who was the Master of the Wardrobe. The house was burnt down in the Great Fire.

Warwick Square, Warwick Lane, EC4

Although the area was re-built in the 1970s to house the latest extensions to the Central Criminal Courts –

(Below) Warwick Square and (right) the Warwick plaque in Newgate Street

the Old Bailey – the name originates from more ancient owners of the land, the Earls of Warwick. On the corner of the lane with Newgate Street is a seventeenth-century tablet commemorating their possessions.

Waterloo Place, SW1

Carlton House was demolished in 1827 and in its grounds the present street system was laid out, including Waterloo Place, which commemorates the great victory of the first Duke of Wellington over Napoleon at Waterloo in 1815.

Watling Street, EC4

When the Romans conquered Britain they built a system of roads so that their armies might travel wherever they were needed as quickly as possible. One of these Roman roads has become known as Watling Street, although there is no evidence that the Romans ever gave it any name. It was the Saxons who called it a 'noble way', using their word *atheling*, which became *Wathing* and then Watling.

Waterloo Place

Weighhouse Street, W1
The King's Weigh House Chapel was originally in Little Cheapside in the City: the congregation moved here in 1891. Once it was called Chandler Street and described the traders here.

Wellington Street, WC2
It is hardly surprising to find a street dedicated to the Iron Duke, especially one leading to Waterloo Bridge.

Well Street, E9
Medicinal wells and springs around London drew people to their waters from far and wide.

Well Walk, NW3
This is perhaps the most celebrated spot in Hampstead, for here was the famous watering place which drew crowds that rivalled those at Bath and Tunbridge Wells.

Wentworth Street, E1
Thomas Wentworth, Lord Chamberlain at the time of Edward VI, had a residence in the vicinity.

Westbourne Terrace, Westbourne Grove, W2
Rising to the north of Paddington, near where Henry VIII hunted and where he later gave two hundred acres to Catharine Parr, the river Westbourne was the bourne (stream) in the west of London.

Westminster
The word 'minster' means a large church, not necessarily a cathedral, but especially a church built on a site associated with the early missionaries. London's largest church was its cathedral, St Paul's in the City, while up stream to the west stood the minster.

Weston Street, SE1
John Webbe Weston owned and lived in the so-called Manor of the Maze here in the early nineteenth century.

Whetstone Park, WC2
William Whetstone, a tobacco overseer at the time of Charles I, traded at the Black Boy in Holborn. In the seventeenth century the park gained a reputation for immorality.

Whitcomb Street, WC2

Formerly called Hedge Lane, a reminder of the once rural scene, the street's present name first appears on maps in the last decades of the seventeenth century. It is named after the speculative builder, William Whitcomb.

Whitechapel High Street, E1

Just outside the City wall, in a hamlet of Stepney, a medieval chapel of white stone stood beside the highway.

Whitefriars Street, EC4

The street originally ran from Fleet Street to the river and was called Water Lane, but after the re-aligning and renaming of streets in 1844 it became Whitefriars. The Carmelite friars, who wore white habits, were established here in 1241 and remained until the dissolution in 1538.

Whitehall, SW1

The street as we know it today is a new alignment of an older one, King Street. Until the sixteenth century Whitehall is referred to as York House or Place, having been given to the Archbishops of York by Hubert de Kent. Then it was acquired by Henry VIII from Cardinal Wolsey and afterwards became known as Whitehall.

White Horse Street, W1

At the accession of George I to the throne of the United Kingdom of England and Scotland the white horse of Hanover became a popular inn sign. On the corner of Piccadilly and this street there stood a tavern with this name. The street twists and turns, running over the line of the river Tyburn.

White Kennett Street, E1

Dean and later Bishop of Peterborough, White Kennett was Rector of St Botolph's church, Aldgate, from 1700 to 1707. He was an opponent of the authority of Convocation and a founder member of the Society for the Propagation of the Gospel.

Whittington Avenue, EC3

Bought from the Neville family by Sir Richard Whittington, the manor of Leadenhall stood on the site of today's market. Whittington Avenue leads from the market to Leadenhall Street.

Wigmore Street, W1

This was so named after Wigmore Castle, in Herefordshire, the ancient seat of the Earls of Oxford, owners of the land here.

Wild Street, WC2
Humphrey Weld built Weld House here in 1640. Wild is a corruption of his name.

William IV Street, WC2
William IV succeeded his brother, George IV, in 1830.

Wilton Crescent, Wilton Place, Wilton Row, SW1
The father-in-law of the first Marquess of Westminster, the first Earl of Wilton, lends his name to these streets.

Winchester Street, Winchester Square, Winchester Yard, SE1
For many centuries the Bishops of Winchester, in whose diocese Southwark was once included, lived in and owned the liberty of the Clink here, outside the jurisdiction of the City of London.

Windmill Hill, NW3
A survey of 1680 shows a windmill on this hill.

Wine Office Court, EC4
The office that dealt with licences to sell wines was sited here.

Winnett Street, W1
In 1935 the London County Council rationalised its street names, renaming some streets. Upper Rupert Street became Winnett Street, named after an alderman of Westminster who had his business here.

Wolsey Mews, NW5
This was built on land once owned by Christ Church, the Oxford college founded by Cardinal Wolsey as Cardinal's College in the sixteenth century, and the mews bears the founder's name.

Woodfall Street, N4
William Woodfall, House of Commons reporter and pioneer of the Hansard reports, lived in Islington.

Wood Street, EC2
Though the street is shown as 'Wodestrate' as early as 1156, opinion differs as to the exact meaning of the word in this instance. Firewood was apparently sold here, objects such as tables were made here, and many of the wooden frames of houses in various parts of the City may have been fashioned here.

Woronzow Road, NW8
A Muscovite, Simon Count Woronzow, former Ambassador to the Court of St James, settled in St Marylebone. On his death in 1827 he left £500 for the poor of the parish. The almshouses in St John's Wood Terrace still bear witness to his generosity.

Wren Street, WC1
Sir Christopher Wren, the architect of St Paul's Cathedral and many other buildings, lived in a house in Holborn.

Wright's Lane, W8
This lane, running beside High Street Kensington station, is named after Gregory Wright, who built houses here *c.*1774.

XX Place, E1
On one of the houses there is an inscription which shows a half-barrel marked XX and bearing the initials I.S.J.S. and the date 1823. Possibly the landlord was a cooper by trade.

Yarmouth Place, W1
The town house of the Earl of Yarmouth was situated here; he died at Dorchester House in 1842.

Yeo Street, E3
Alfred Yeo was a member of the Poplar District Board of Works and later served on the London County Council.

York Buildings, York Place, WC2
In the sixteenth century the London house of the Archbishops of York was here, by the river's edge.

York Road, SW11 and SW18
In Tudor times the Archbishops of York had a country house here, built by Archbishop Laurence between 1476 and 1480.

York Street, W1
Frederick, Duke of York and Albany, brother of George IV, is remembered here.

Zoar Street, SE1
The street is called after a chapel where John Bunyan preached.

Index